Cold Email

Marketing

How to Build a Profitable Email List That Pays Forever

(How to Fill Your Sales Pipeline, Convert Like Crazy and Level Up Your Business)

Nancy Meyers

Published By **Andrew Zen**

Nancy Meyers

Cold Email Marketing: How to Build a Profitable Email List That Pays Forever (How to Fill Your Sales Pipeline, Convert Like Crazy and Level Up Your Business)

ISBN 978-1-998901-24-1

Legal & Disclaimer

The information contained in this ebook is not designed to replace or take the place of any form of medicine or professional medical advice. The information in this ebook has been provided for educational & entertainment purposes only.

The information contained in this book has been compiled from sources deemed reliable, and it is accurate to the best of the Author's knowledge; however, the Author cannot guarantee its accuracy and validity and cannot be held liable for any errors or omissions. Changes are periodically made to this book. You must consult your doctor or get professional medical advice before using any of the suggested remedies, techniques, or information in this book.

Upon using the information contained in this book, you agree to hold harmless the Author from and against any damages, costs, and expenses, including any legal fees potentially resulting from the application of any of the information provided by this guide. This disclaimer applies to any damages or injury caused by the use and application, whether directly or indirectly, of any advice or information presented, whether for breach of contract, tort, negligence, personal injury, criminal intent, or under any other cause of action.

You agree to accept all risks of using the information presented inside this book. You need to consult a professional medical practitioner in order to ensure you are both able and healthy enough to participate in this program.

Table Of Contents

Chapter 1: Sending Emails In Today's Digital Landscape

Email marketing and advertising is arguably your unmarried most treasured on line commercial enterprise organization asset.

Yet email advertising and advertising isn't as smooth or as smooth as hitting "supply" after which calling it a day. When you're doing it proper, as advertising and advertising and advertising and marketing and advertising cartoonist Tom Fishburne said4, "the top notch advertising and marketing doesn't enjoy like advertising and marketing". This declaration is especially relevant to the manner you're showing up in the inbox.

When someone symptoms and symptoms and signs and symptoms up for your e-mail listing, you may't cope with that subscriber's inbox as even though it's your non-public billboard; rather, it's your possibility to construct relationships and connections. It's your functionality to find out that balance with the way you're selling your self and the way you're connecting together with your subscribers at the manner to play a massive characteristic in defining your fulfillment as an email marketer.

While your marketing and connection capabilities are a top element, they aren't the only factors.

Your capability to capitalize on what works well for you and to ditch what doesn't may even play a large function. To do this, you'll should know your numbers.

Now, in advance than you provide me the road that you "aren't a numbers individual" or inform me that you "suck at math" - cool story, bruh! If you noticed how commonly I sweat thru and second-guessed all the re-calculations I ran for the examples in this book, we'd have a chuckle.

The cause I blanketed these type of examples - and the book is full of them! - is to offer you the opportunity to appearance what the numbers can do for you, and you can 100% "suck at math" however nonetheless be able to see and recognize styles for your advertising and advertising and marketing efforts.

Usually, the issues with small on-line business commercial enterprise enterprise owners not believing they may be analytical is due to the fact their reviews are a cluttered, overwhelming mess. And #sorrynotsorry however messy opinions aren't going to inspire you to do something aside from log the heck off; it's dang-close to not possible to get facts-driven and to optimize any of your marketing and advertising and marketing campaigns at the identical time as you can't even see your outcomes, an lousy lot much much less make experience of them.

With Email Marketing Optimization, we're going to cowl some nice practices for sending and publishing your emails, we're going to set up the form of monitoring an notable manner to present you those clear opinions you may use to get records-pushed, and we're going to spell the whole thing out for you, out of your campaigns, to your optimization strategies, for your problem-shooting.

But before we can do any of that, we need first of all what your crook and moral duties are as an e mail marketer.

LEGAL COMPLIANCE IN EMAIL MARKETING

Getting legally compliant with the manner you're sending e-mail sounds intimidating… till you begin doing it. Then you understand that maximum of it's miles commonplace feel and all of it is based on getting email entrepreneurs to behave and have interaction like real humans who have been raised to be polite and to be kind to every different. (Yes, even on-line!)

Which is some thing we are able to all get at the back of, n'est-ce pas?

Before we get into an appropriate prison hints that impact your e-mail advertising and marketing and marketing practices, let's begin with the maximum important detail of any electronic mail you deliver: widely recognized that you're connecting with someone or girls and that they will be the most important a part of this whole interplay.

As such, the legal guidelines you have to abide with the resource of aren't the criminal guidelines which you, the sender, are ruled through. Instead, it is the legal pointers that govern the recipient that you want to obey on the same time as you're sending electronic mail to them. It makes enjoy in case you bear in mind it due to the truth those prison recommendations are mounted location to defend the purchaser and almost about electronic mail advertising and advertising, the recipient is the client.

Does this imply that you are expected to paste to the laws that govern each special nationality you have were given to your email listing? Well, certainly high-quality, that IS the expectancy. However, you don't must join up into regulation university or end up an international privateness professional or some thing to do this.

There's lots of overlap with what the ones laws cowl and that makes feel. After all, the motive and recognition for a number of those criminal hints is to shield the client, and no matter wherein the law is coming from, the methods to try this have a whole lot more in commonplace than they'll be terrific.

The TL;DR for this is in case you stay via way of way of the motto "don't be a grossy-pants marketer", you are likely nicely. But simply in case, allow's walk you thru what that truely method and a number of the procedures "being a remarkable human inside the inbox" is legislated.

If you've got got any precise questions or unique problems approximately this, I should encourage you to are searching out out propose from each a attorney or privacy expert who specializes in this vicinity to provide you with individualized feedback.

GDPR

Just like song competition posters begin with the beneficial resource of putting their headlining acts as an awful lot as in huge formidable letters, we're going to take the equal approach right here and begin our communique about email law with the

European Union's General Data Protection Regulation, or what the cool children like us check with as GDPR.

If you've got got been within the virtual advertising worldwide decrease lower back in the spring of 2018, you'll bear in mind the right now-up "fowl little, sky is falling" vibes even as it modified into shared that GDPR might be enforced and all people had higher fall in line however brief.

While the purpose for all this panic changed into the belief that GDPR could constitute "the cease of e-mail advertising and advertising and marketing", it might be in the path of truth to say that GDPR could possibly complicate the potential for spammers and unethical marketers to send out email to those who didn't want or who didn't agree to receiving this e-mail in the first location. Despite hundreds of initial sentiment that GDPR modified into "anti-commercial enterprise organization", the enforcement changed into surely "pro-consumer" and it placed problems like "consent" on the center of revised digital advertising and advertising practices.

As such, the quit end result modified into that in case you were collecting electronic mail addresses from European Union (EU) residents, you needed to benefit explicit consent. Anyone from the EU whose e mail deal with you had been collecting could need to simply accept the clean preference to agree or disagree to having their personal statistics collected. Email marketers were anticipated to provide the motive for which this information was being collected and might be used. Individuals can also moreover be granted enterprise as to how marketers used their statistics and within the event that they selected to not be on an email touch listing, GDPR tips country that marketers have to offer with a easy way for subscribers to pick out out of further communications thru manner of an "unsubscribe" button or link.

For most e mail entrepreneurs, it wasn't in reality absolutely well worth the trouble of seeking to phase their EU subscribers from the relaxation of the area. For what GDPR changed into imposing, it made greater revel in to take an "across the board" method as it blanketed logical and moral practices collectively with:

- Obtaining consent from email subscribers to advantage further conversation;

- The responsibility for email entrepreneurs in case you want to find out and communicate how an person's touch facts come to be acquired; and

- Providing electronic mail subscribers with the selection and agency to control their subscription settings interior each email that is despatched.

GDPR turn out to be basically the internet equal of being capable of ask a cellphone solicitor to "please take away me from your name listing."

Canada's Anti-Spam Legislation

While GDPR is the maximum famous teen inside the elegance of e-mail advertising regulation, it wasn't the primary infant at the block.

In 2014, Canada's Anti-Spamming Legislation turn out to be surpassed and due to the fact every brilliant regulation loves a excellent acronym, this one is typically referred to as CASL. In the summer season of 2018, truely after GDPR modified into enforced, the Spam Reporting Center recorded greater than 137,000 junk mail complaints5. The pinnacle purpose for the ones court cases have emerge as said to be the receipt of emails to which they did now not consent to receiving. There had been also court docket docket times approximately the rise of textual content message unsolicited mail, which I definitely have every motive to accept as true with may be a growing style.

We will communicate masses more approximately unsolicited mail throughout this book, and the manner you could avoid being categorised as a spammer (ew!). However, there's moreover quite some excellent extra records to be had in this difficulty at fightspam.Gc.Ca, if that's some aspect you're inquisitive about exploring in addition.

But that same theme of "obtaining consent" is at the leading aspect all all over again with CASL as it's far for GDPR, further to offering clarity as to who the sender of the emails are. This way that as an e-mail marketer in compliance to CASL, you want your emails to encompass:

● A "from" area that certainly suggests who the sender of this e-mail is;

● An sincere avenue and/or mailing address in which the sender may be reached; and

● A use of hassle traces that is not designed to be deceptive, misleading or dishonest.

On a non-public be conscious, I don't need to stay in a international - now not even a virtual one! - wherein those aren't famous as baseline courtesies every body apprehend and adopt. Think of your self as a client and I bet you experience the same due to the fact knowing who you're shopping for from, a manner to the touch them and making sincere claims about what they have to offer sincerely isn't an excessive amount of to invite.

This is a exercise I inspire you to do as often as viable: do not forget what you'll want and recognize as a customer in place of setting your advertising needs and goals first.

CAN-SPAM Act

The Federal Trade Commission (FTC) changed into the first to enact a rustic massive fashionable for the distribution of commercial enterprise electronic mail with the CAN-SPAM Act in 2003. It's legit call is a hint extra of a mouthful because it stands for the Controlling the Assault of Non-Solicitied Pornography and Marketing Act of 2003.

While the Act doesn't reference acquiring express consent, it touches on maximum great objects we've already stated like offering a bodily deal with, presenting the selection to determine-out of communique, and keeping off using deceptive or misleading situation traces.

It additionally stipulates that if a message is certainly an commercial, the sender is wanted to make it clear that the message is, in reality, an commercial. This includes another framing you may use for cash or merchandise you got in alternate for sharing that message, which incorporates associate commissions or logo sponsorships.

In quick, if you're getting a bit some thing-some element in trade for sending a message out, CAN-SPAM compliance obliges you to reveal this truth.

There also are many one-of-a-kind related crook recommendations overlaying many particular countries and regions. For example, the California Consumer Privacy Act (additionally known as CCPA) protects California us of a citizens a good buy in the way GDPR protects EU residents.

I inspire you to examine up and studies the ones subjects similarly and to speak with a prison and/or privateness expert for any problems you can have.

However, there are a whole lot of commonplace troubles and overlap, and the maximum huge versions are commonly in what constitutes a breach regular with which law and to what degree the penalty is enforced.

Because positive, you'll be proper to mention this. As I referred to earlier, those laws aren't "anti-commercial company" however rather, they're placed to be "seasoned-patron". They offer e mail entrepreneurs with a baseline of right ethics with how we're emailing and talking with our audience.

And look, there's continually "that one individual" who ruins it extreme approximately the rest parents and that's what the ones laws had to be installed location for; it's because of the fact no longer every body sees these baselines because of the fact the form of respectful verbal exchange to which we ought to all be entitled to and guardrails therefore need to be installed region and enforced.

Once once more, I remind you which you'd be hard-pressed to take a prison incorrect turn in case you make a difficulty of re-framing all your e-mail advertising and advertising and advertising efforts across the questions like "What should I like and what should I want to collect as a customer? How do I need to be spoken to and communicated with? What obstacles should I want others to understand?"

CHOOSING EMAIL MARKETING SOFTWARE

Now that we've got a few readability as to what we're legally sure to embody in our emails, permit's communicate approximately the way you're going to get the ones emails despatched.

There are a variety of alternatives almost about choosing an electronic mail advertising provider business enterprise, or what the cool youngsters name an EMS. Instead of focusing at the man or woman electronic mail marketing provider options available to you, I'll draw your interest to what you'll need to search for and take into account in advance than deciding on one:

• They comply to privateness law;

The handiest manner to pick out out if your EMS prioritizes privateness compliance is to appearance their earnings internet page and expertise base for the time period "GDPR". Every responsible and worthwhile e-mail advertising and marketing and marketing carrier should offer records about how their software software complies to GDPR and it ought to offer guidance to its clients as to how they may and ought to be compliant with their practices the usage of its platform.

- They ask you to validate your gift contacts;

If you already have some contacts to add and that they ask you to offer information as to the way you obtained these contacts, that's a splendid signal. Sure, it's a pain inside the rear to validate your listing, however trust me, it's a remarkable signal.

Why? Because it technique that spammy game enthusiasts are being restricted in their capability to get right of entry to that tool and rent that platform.

In flip, this indicates your service's servers - the equal servers your emails may be going via - are lots lots much less probable to be flagged for sending spammy content material. It blessings you for your email marketing enterprise to be selective about who they serve because of the truth what every body else does and sends thru the servers you all percent can effect your deliverability thru proxy.

• They require you to use a internet site-based definitely truely email;

You don't want to be coping with an e-mail advertising and marketing and advertising and advertising and marketing service who will will let you use your @gmail.Com address for the equal motives as above: your emails will be sharing and using the same servers as your electronic mail marketing business enterprise's customers do. That's why it's vital that you be affiliated with official folks that, at least, are willing to spend money on owning a domain name from which they will do organization.

• They allow for tagging and segmentation.

I hold forth the price of sending your human beings emails they in truth need to open and take a look at. That's why you need the functionality to tag and section, and which you use your tags and segments to deliver emails which can be precise and relevant to every subscriber.

We'll communicate extra about what segmentation is and a few awesome practices a little later in this module, however that is a characteristic you in truth want your e-mail advertising and advertising and marketing company to embody.

My final advice even as choosing an email advertising and advertising and advertising service has less to do with the software itself and further with the manner you need or plan to characteristic: take into account whether or no longer you want an all-in-one tool or if you'd instead a stand-on my own platform.

An all-in-one tool would possibly residence everything you need to characteristic your online corporation. In my case, I sell courses and virtual downloads, which means that I want a course hosting platform, video website hosting, profits pages, fee processing, pick out

out-in forms, an affiliate application and, of direction, e mail advertising. For me, it makes experience to apply an all-in-one answer an fantastic manner to permit me to connect all of the shifting quantities internal my operations without counting on an outdoor automation tool like Zapier to keep the whole lot linked. I additionally benefit from having the analytics for each of those covered, because of this that that key records points like "subscriber fee" (which we can see in addition in Module 2) are generated for me automatically.

The downsides of the use of this form of all-in-one platform is that you can count on a steep analyzing curve and it can seem expensive even as you're clearly starting out. Of course, if you're already buying maximum of these terrific services one after the opposite, the fee is there.

I'm for my part a large fan of Kartra and it's what I use to run my online employer. You can visit ebook.Omgrowth.Com/email for a 14-day trial to check it out and explore if it might be a first-rate healthful for you.

Someone on foot a simpler operation may additionally choose to use a stand-by myself platform that they're able to combine with the opposite tools they use.

These can be an lousy lot a great deal much less steeply-priced than an all-in-one solution, and that they have got an inclination to be less tough to investigate and use.

The most well-known services often "play nicely with others" as they are intended to hook up with super services that small industrial company owners like yourself can be using and could gain from connecting to so that you can more efficiently tag your leads based on how they have interaction together along with your extraordinary merchandise and assets.

In the beyond, I've used ConvertKit and it's what I would possibly go again to the use of if I have been seeking out a stand-on my own e-mail marketing provider. It's a platform that's simple sufficient to quick get commenced with, and but strong sufficient to develop with you.

There's no "right" or "wrong" preference, but there is a choice that is proper for you and the way you need to operate. Each EMS will snap its suspenders as to which competencies it has to provide and the manner they study to their competition. It's all-too-clean to get "the grass is greener" syndrome where you're hopping from one service to every other however coping with all the ones statistics transfers is a waste of some time and strength that would be better invested in serving your target market.

Choosing some thing you may find the money for, some issue with a purpose to accommodate each your present day requirements in addition to permitting room on your boom, whilst moreover making sure that it complies to the criminal suggestions and ethics of on-line industrial business agency and electronic mail deliverability.

TAGGING AND SEGMENTING

I said that tagging and segmenting is one of the deal-breaker skills you will need with any email marketing and advertising carrier you pick out.

Let's get into why it's crucial and some of the approaches you can technique this.

WHAT IS EMAIL SEGMENTATION?

You have a mean email list however as a manner to start sending hyper-focused emails to the proper those who may be most open and receptive to receiving what you're sharing in those emails, you want to undertake a exercise that is referred to as "electronic mail segmentation". This takes place on the identical time as you divide that commonplace contacts into smaller, greater defined corporations, or segments.

"But Lanie!", you can say. "I most effective speak about one component. All of my subscribers percentage the perfect same, single interest." Cool beans! That simplifies topics... however you still need to phase your target market based totally on wherein they are of their interactions with you.

For example, in the occasion that they already supplied the provide you're going to remind your listing about next week, you each a) don't need to ship the ones promotional emails to that phase of your target audience who already purchased it, or b) you need to send a modified model that reminds your clients of the incredible abilties their past buy has that they're able to revisit and hold making the most of.

Tagging and segmenting is sort of a muscle; the more you use it, the extra makes use of you'll find out for it and the stronger your sport can be from placing it to apply.

What is the difference amongst "segments" and "tags"?

This is the sort of "similar however special" requirements in which each terms serve the same reason - in this situation, to understand a selected fine or element of a person - but each is applied in a extremely good manner.

When you section a listing, you're taking the overall contacts to your list to create "micro-lists" primarily based completely mostly on a few thing that defines them and isn't always going to exchange. Meanwhile, while you tag someone for your listing, you're growing reference factors for their choices and behaviors.

I'm a massive fan of examples to colour a photo so allow's use one and say you run a set software program program. You have one electronic mail listing with 2 segments: one phase fabricated from your average listing and each different section for the those who are paid individuals of your software.

Having the ones segments allows you to use your "paid contributors" segment to speak software program-associated information to the folks who are already part of your club at the identical time as you could take your "number one listing" phase to exclude anybody who's inside the "paid contributors" section whilst you're sending promotions that encourage humans to sign up inside the program.

As for tagging, you'll tag humans based totally on pursuits, options and behaviors. What does that appear to be?

Let's push this situation further and say you're on foot a advertising in your club. You now need to conform with-up with folks who confirmed hobby in becoming a member of your club however have not started to take a look at-via; you could tag the individuals who clicked a hyperlink in your promotional emails to go to your profits net internet web page as having proven hobby inside the software.

Furthermore, if you have the only of a kind styles of humans for your target market - say you help health professionals - you could tag your target marketplace based totally on whether or not or no longer they discover as health opposition, personal going for walks shoes or logo fashions/ambassadors. This will assist you to hyper-customize your messages and promotions to those 3 tremendous interest businesses you serve and adapt your message to the specific incentives you can offer every interest group has to sign up for.

Think of your segments due to the fact the overarching lists which incorporates the contacts you promote to, your clients after which your friends, even as your tags are greater hobby- and conduct-primarily based virtually equipment to help you outline and come to be privy to elements of your subscribers as a way to better equip you to serve them.

Let's turn this example right into a case take a look at of a person who uses your segments to demonstrate their communication opportunities.

Someone subscribes on your listing, which populates them into your "normal promo" section. They take a quiz that identifies them as a "brand ambassador", this is an identifier you tag them with.

They pass directly to go to your income page and they attend some of your workshops, all of which can be behaviors you moreover can also moreover tagged them with.

Because you sent focused emails to people who confirmed interest within the product, this individual in the long run did purchase your product and you may then add them on your segment of clients. In fact, they loved your product hundreds that they signed as an lousy lot as emerge as an associate, this is every specific phase they've been delivered to.

Meanwhile, their brand ambassador popularity way they've got an inbox so cluttered and busy, even the messiest youngster would be vital. Your subscriber decided to de-clutter their inbox and that they've selected to pick out out of receiving further promotional emails from you, but further they need to maintain receiving companion and product updates.

Had you not segmented this individual, they'll have unsubscribed in reality out of your e mail list. This may additionally additionally need to get messy after they attempted to access their buy another time but couldn't after unsubscribing, and it could fee you a few word-of-mouth income your partner software can also have otherwise endured sharing with them.

Had you no longer tagged this individual, you could not have identified enough about this character to craft the hyper-centered message for logo ambassadors who already showed interest in the product that resulted within the sale of your product, and the subsequent accomplice income they introduced to you as nicely.

Establishing a strategic technique to the way you phase and tag your subscribers will devour some of a while, energy and mind vicinity, but the above instance need to reveal the price in doing so for both your subscribers similarly on your private backside line.

SEGMENTATION AND TAGGING STRATEGIES

I've already alluded to a number of the techniques in which you can section your list so permit's start with the ones:

PURCHASE SEGMENTS

As a baseline, you want to create a phase for the shoppers of every of your gives and there are some motives for this.

The first motive is if a person includes a choice they want to unsubscribe from your advertising substances however they want to maintain receiving updates on a product they offered from you, growing this form of segmentation will empower them to do that.

You might also grumble approximately not being able to pitch new offers to them, however this may be a short-sighted view. Someone who desires to preserve receiving product updates is absolutely satisfied with the product they bought. They won't want to pay attention about your gives anymore but they nevertheless want in on what you've delivered to their table and that has price. After all, the ones are the types of people you could assume for word-of-mouth; the possibility to collect out to them to allow them to realize you've up to date some detail they already have been given price from is also an possibility to be the the front-of-mind for a moment, it certainly is all-the-extra motive to maintain appealing collectively together with your shoppers after the purchase and to avoid making an investment your complete email advertising and marketing efforts on genuinely income and pitches.

Another motive you need to section your customers is for a reason that become touched on already: whilst you're promoting a suggestion they've already offered, you don't want to pitch this section with some aspect they've got already paid you for. However, that doesn't recommend you could't moreover electronic mail the ones subscribers at some point of this time.

The difference is that at the same time as you're sending emails that pitch your product to non-consumers, it's a fantastic possibility to replace that messaging out for the folks that already sold your offer and allow them to understand that may be a wonderful time to sign up for your companion software program software to make profits within the route of this promotional duration, or to remind them of updates or adjustments you've made to the product that they may want to revisit and maintain receiving price from.

And sooner or later, thru segmenting your clients, it is much less difficult so that it will personalize upsell and downsell messages based mostly on wherein they've already invested. For instance, in case you're selling a modern offer, you may write a greater focused e-mail that speaks at once to those who've some enjoy together with your merchandise versus what you may write to the ones who have never provided some thing from you.

You want your human beings to experience visible. You want your people to revel in like you're associated and assembly them in which they are in desire to in fact selling them what you need them to shop for. You want your human beings to experience like they're valued and they aren't "without a doubt some other email deal with" you market to.

The satisfactory manner to acquire this is to place a while, strive and purpose inside the again of "seeing" and segmenting your customers intentionally and as it have to be.

AFFILIATE SEGMENTS

Affiliates are humans who've raised their hand and stated "I'll vouch for you and your offers!".

The idea is that within the occasion that they direct purchasers closer to your offers like air website site visitors control, you can thank them with the resource of manner of paying out a fee or accomplice charge whenever they acquire this.

It's a splendid concept to both tag or better however, segment those subscribers from your electronic mail listing due to the fact the verbal exchange you percentage with them may be very one-of-a-kind from your "normal" emails. In truth, you can have people segmented as friends for your listing who are not and don't need to be subscribed to your promotions and gives, and you need to address that. After all, it is probably a disgrace to deter a person from offering you with "on line road cred" once they spread the word about you, simply because of the fact they aren't interested by receiving your promotional emails.

In any case, you will be sending emails to this organisation about your promotions however the messaging of the emails you deliver to this phase may be very one-of-a-kind from the ones you ship the rest of your listing. First of all, you could normally be letting this segment comprehend of promotions earlier of time a good way to prepare to promote them in advance than your essential electronic mail list even is aware about about it. You'll probable moreover be sharing folders of done-for-you promotional materials like social media snap shots and swipe duplicate so that you can help your pals promote your offers and those are materials you wouldn't proportion together together with your number one email listing.

That's why it's miles a brilliant concept to hold a phase of your list this is separate and dedicated to your affiliate subscribers because the way you communicate with them is likewise separate and dedicated.

For maximum online groups, your customers and your buddies further on your promotional contact list is probably what make up your segments, and the entirety listed beneath might be tags.

However, the ones are recommendations, there may be no "rule" about this. Remember which you're the boss, apple sauce. This manner you recognize your industrial organisation higher than every person, you get to make the alternatives as to the manner you enjoy your subscribers are wonderful identified and the manner your agency version excellent operates and must be defined.

IDENTIFIER TAGS

I used the earlier example of a corporation serving health experts with a couple of sub-classes for the humans it serves, which include

 health competitors, personal walking footwear and emblem models/ambassadors.

With a number of the primary few emails you supply, you can ask your new subscribers to self-discover and tag them therefore. This permits you to no longer best create greater centered communications however it moreover offers you with deeper insights as to what your target market includes, which also can have an impact at the manner you pick out to market your self with paid commercials, social media messaging or even your offers.

Another method to have interaction and get subscribers to self-perceive is with a quiz. A quiz can be used as a lead magnet that encourages humans to join up on your e-mail list, but it may moreover assist you hone in on the ones pursuits and traits you need to tag and aim.

While employer or challenge become aware of is one vicinity in which your humans can self-choose out, different factors you can recollect tagging are their desires, their values, their vicinity, their way of life, their reviews, or their gender, absolutely to name a few.

Keep in mind that the ones are really examples and you don't need to be gathering private data you don't want and can't use.

For instance, if your offers aren't geo-centric, then you definitely don't want to be collecting data approximately their area whilst you're in no way going to absolutely use it. However, in case you run a t-shirt keep with more than one places that each has its private sports and promotions, it would be applicable on the manner to gather this person's area to higher hold them knowledgeable of the activities taking area at their network keep.

ENGAGEMENT TAGS

You also can tag human beings based totally on how they're engaging on the facet of your communications and gives. For instance, you'll tag people based totally on which decide-ins or lead magnets they've signed up to enroll in on your e-mail list and you could tag unique hyperlinks they clicked-via to your emails and/or pages they visited.

How your subscribers are engaging at the side of your brand and its content material can be precious statistics. How? Because you can use that statistics to:

● Determine the conversion fees for wonderful forms of subscribers and hone in on how and why unique sorts of subscribers convert to income higher than others;

• Assess the recognition of specific offers - every paid and unfastened - in addition to the following engagement levels you count on primarily based on a subscriber's interests, attendance or engagement;

• Follow up with subscribers who didn't buy your offer, but engaged with/confirmed interest for your promotional substances; and

• Identify tendencies in the way you're presently selling that you could parlay into future advertising campaigns to peer better consequences together with your subsequent efforts.

OPT-IN TAGS

It's a amazing concept, on every occasion feasible, to tag how humans came onto your list. You can and ought to anticipate to peer wildly numerous engagement ranges based totally totally on how human beings placed you and joined your e mail listing.

For example, a joint project wherein someone else vouched to your statistics will enchantment to a considered one among a kind form of subscriber than your paid advert campaigns may want to.

Likewise, folks who opted into your list to down load a PDF will usually show off precise behaviors than the those who opted-in to a workshop in which you dropped all of the information bombs.

This use of tags may be useful at the equal time as you're looking to turn out to be privy to tendencies in pastimes and behaviors from people who've already sold from you. This way, you may with out trouble emerge as privy to those free offers you want to put in front of people you're trying to warmth up previous to launching and you can select out which pick-ins aren't supporting your enterprise the way you want them to with reference to engagement or unsubscribe prices.

ENGAGEMENT LEVEL TAGS

Another element surely worth monitoring is HOW engaged a subscriber is. If a person isn't reading or enticing together along with your emails, that's a trouble and it's one you want to deal with.

You don't want humans ignoring your emails and you virtually don't want to be identifying to shop for the "privilege" to benefit this. Because right here's the reality of it: the more subscribers you have on your e mail listing, the higher the carrier charges are from your e mail advertising service. That's truly one of the many reasons why you don't need to carry human beings thru as subscribers in the occasion that they're simply deleting and/or ignoring your emails.

Another key cause you don't want to preserve unengaged subscribers in your e mail listing is due to the fact it may impact the deliverability of your emails. We'll talk about this greater in Module 2 however when your deliverability fees are impacted, it manner that the folks that in reality need to get preserve of your emails either a) obtained't reap them at all or b) you'll come to be in their junk mail folder in place of their inbox.

That's why you keep tabs on the engagement degree of your subscribers and once they obtain a certain component of disengagement, you can then take movement to every re-engage them or unsubscribe them in your e-mail listing because you've showed that they aren't interested in your communications any in addition. We'll also find out re-engagement sequences and the manner they paintings in Module 3 but earlier than you may re-interact your subscribers, you'll need to prioritize maintaining tabs on their engagement ranges within the first area.

Since we're near engagement, permit's communicate about what you're doing to get your email subscribers engaged.

GETTING YOUR EMAILS READ

It is my opinion that one of the worst subjects you may do collectively at the side of your e-mail listing is to teach your subscribers to dismiss your emails.

Giving your subscribers the possibility to determine-out of a particular promoting or self-pick out precise subjects they're not interested in being attentive to approximately is an unnoticed tactic of electronic mail advertising. When you deliver humans an possibility to speak up about what they aren't inquisitive about hearing about inside the meanwhile, you're lessening the opportunities of having your emails sit down down in their inbox, being overlooked.

You have the ones, proper? When you got an e-mail promoting some component you're now not interested in and also you need to stay on that individual's e mail listing. But you start ignoring their following couple of emails because you're aware about it's probable approximately that one offer you're not interested in.

By no longer giving your subscribers the choice to determine-out of a selected advertising, you're schooling human beings to begin ignoring your emails. The unfortunate element is this dependancy of ignoring your emails has a excessive threat of lasting longer than your promoting will.

Don't train your e mail subscribers to push aside you. Instead, be the form of marketer who gives your email subscribers a few commercial enterprise agency approximately what they select to get preserve of from you and in turn, you're much more likely to be the form of marketer whose campaigns continuously experience applicable and whose emails get opened more regularly.

I don't fake to be an expert or expert in writing email reproduction, however I will constantly cheer more-tough for the following little little bit of great-easy recommendation: stop writing and selling like a marketer. Instead, technique what you have got to say from the point of view of the customer.

If someone self-identifies as being subscribed on your podcast, maybe you don't have to harass them with promotions approximately what your podcast episode is ready this week;

they're already subscribed in your podcast and they'll see that facts pop up in their player while you publish a brand new episode. Perhaps a "round-up" fashion e mail once a month will be extra suitable to supply to the ones subscribers, with reachable links to key objects you may have stated in the beyond month's episodes and remind them of associated gives or posts. It might moreover be profitable a remarkable way to hone in on how your engagement with the emails containing that particular messaging are acting in assessment to your exceptional pronounces.

When you've got a have a look at your project line, ask your self the query "could likely I click on on this?" When you examine your e mail, ask your self "may also I be inquisitive about this?" Pull a protracted way from thinking about WHAT you're promoting, and attempt to attention extra on whether or not you're giving your subscribers a purpose to care about your gives, your message and your campaigns. Put the focus on emails which may be in your subscribers' advantage… in desire to putting your backside line and sales dreams first.

There's no motive why this could't or shouldn't be a mutually beneficial relationship.

Writing emails that gets opened is a skills all on its private and even as I hobby on monitoring and enhancing the general common performance for the emails you hit deliver on, you may visit e-book.Omgrowth.Com/electronic mail for my personal hints of folks that rock socks at schooling on-line marketers collectively with you a way to decorate your actual email copywriting skills and level-up your content material fabric fabric improvement recreation.

We've pointed out the content material material you're publishing, your criminal obligations, what to search for in an email advertising issuer further to some of the techniques you can higher segment and target your subscribers.

Let's flow onto WHAT you're monitoring approximately your subscribers and electronic mail overall performance, and the manner you're going to do this.

Chapter 2: Tracking Your Emails Like They Owe You Money

I'm going to begin this communique with the notion that whether or not or no longer or no longer you understand the number one aspect approximately using it, you do have analytics software program hooked up on and monitoring your net website on-line.

If you want help selecting which platform to choose, you can take note of episodes 53 and fifty four of the OMGrowth Podcast or visit e-book.Omgrowth.Com/e mail to get Results On Repeat, my ebook on monitoring and optimizing your normal virtual advertising and advertising overall performance.

I say this because of the reality, fantastic, your electronic mail advertising and marketing issuer does acquire some precious facts for you... but what takes place inside the inbox is most effective one a part of the story you care to file on.

Your e mail advertising and advertising and marketing and advertising service collects information about how people are attractive with the emails themselves. What it could't inform you, even though, is what your people are doing after the clicking-via on that e-mail. What are your e mail subscribers doing after they click on-thru to your internet website online? How are they navigating your pages and your gives? What varieties of moves are they taking once they get there and the manner prolonged are they staying?

That's wherein your internet site analytics comes into play because it will record on things you want to recognise like which net website online pages or offers did your subscribers go to beyond that first click on on-via.

How engaged had been they together along with your content cloth once they reach it?

Did they do what you favored them to do when they have been given for your internet web page? Did they look at the income page? Did they watch the video? Did they click at the checkout button? Did they purchase your offer?

Was one e-mail much more likely to make the sale for you than some different?

Was one electronic mail greater appealing than some different?

Were there tremendous variations some of the emails that observed the maximum engagement rather than individuals who generated the most earnings?

What tendencies are you capable of choose out approximately your most-changing emails, and how will you reflect the ones favorable results more often?

You can answer all of these questions and extra on the same time as you're intentional approximately monitoring the whole photograph of your email advertising effects, and at the same time as you apprehend exactly what your numbers are telling you about what your subsequent nice circulate is.

EMAIL MARKETING METRICS

A metric is something that you degree and can function a numbered price to that lets in you to represent the outcome of some thing particular you're doing. An instance of this may be your click-thru charge, this means that the proportion of subscribers you despatched an electronic mail to who clicked on a link within that electronic mail.

Metrics are like people: we're no longer speculated to be isolated however we do want "by myself time" to deliver our fantastic selves to the desk. This is why you'll degree your metrics in isolation but your effects will shine brightest while you deliver different factors into play with it.

Let's live along with your click on-via charge as an example of a metric: you acquired't be making any agency selections based on looking totally at your click on-through price and also you received't be measuring any type of achievement in competition to that one facts issue. After all, your click on on-thru fee may be immoderate because quite some human beings were clicking in your "unsubscribe" button and that would not often be what you'll name a fulfillment intention.

Meanwhile, take that same click on on-via charge and integrate it together with your conversions to profits from e mail subscribers, and now we're speakme!

Your statistics is meant to be interacted with and on the identical time as your metrics each get measured one at a time, it's the questions and the recollections that your super, innovative mind brings to and builds around these data devices an top notch manner to make your information - and your effects! - shine.

Let's start by way of searching on the metrics that maximum electronic mail marketing services pre-programs and offers for you.

EMAIL MARKETING SERVICE METRICS

OPEN RATES

I need to begin with "open charges" - now not because of the truth it is important however -

due to the fact it's miles nearly useless. Once upon a time, it carried all varieties of price: it have become a hallmark of how many humans have been surely reading (or as a minimum skimming through) your emails, it helped you test out the popularity of your hassle traces, it could moreover be a making plans tool in phrases of figuring out what time of day your subscribers were the most lively.

Those days are behind us and also you'll get masses of finger-pointing inside the route of Apple's iOS replace again in June 2021 as to the motive why. This replace got here with all sorts of privacy abilties, virtually one in every of which protected Mail Privacy Protection that stopped e-mail tracking for Apple mail users until consent to do in any other case changed into furnished. As a plot twist to this blockade, electronic mail entrepreneurs clearly observed increases of their open expenses. Why? Because what Apple implemented didn't virtually block the tracking pixels from tracking however alternatively, those tracking pixels had been pre-loaded; because of this emails that may not have been opened the least bit had those monitoring pixels pre-loaded and therefore inflated e mail open charges past what they clearly were.

TL;DR: Changes in privateness have rendered your open prices as an unreliable metric and goalpost.

Sure, you'll locate advice from human beings telling you that you may however use open fees in case you section your Apple mail customers but that's a brief-term answer. I as a substitute inspire you to just accept the inevitable and to provide your open prices the equal treatment as that date you had been as soon as excited to transport on however in the in the meantime are happy to overlook approximately it ever took place. That's the vibe proper right here.

For all the finger-pointing at Apple for doing this, you could search around and see that is a fashion you'd do better to enroll within the bandwagon on than to withstand. According to Gartner665% of the area's population could have its personal facts covered under contemporary-day privacy rules through the use of 2023, up from 10% in 2020.

Changes are coming from browsers and provider carriers almost about cookie-blocking and proscribing zero.33-birthday party tracking even as global regulation will increasingly more strain marketers to act in a greater moral, privacy-compliant way with how they do enterprise on-line. This is why I insist which you get onboard, adapt to or maybe encompass bizarre thoughts like "consent" - certain! While virtual residents! - because of the reality in an ironic twist of fate, parents that do not get onboard with obtaining consent to accumulate non-public information will always have consent forced upon them.

But as Forbes reassures us7, the cease of open charges is not a trademark of "the give up of email advertising" and the sky isn't falling... But clicks for the time being are the priority metric in the direction of which you could diploma email engagement that subjects.

CLICK-THROUGH RATES

Welcome in your baseline e-mail advertising and advertising and marketing metric that answers the query: "Are my subscribers appealing with the emails I'm sending to them?"

The title ought to describe all of it however what we're talking about is the fee at which your subscribers click-via at the hyperlinks embedded into the emails you deliver.

In the phase we're able to see later known as "Your Email Tracking System", we will look at what you need to put in force to track what takes location AFTER the clicking-via. But for now, we're going to be glad with information that click-throughs are our fundamental place to begin.

A query I frequently get asked is "what's a high-quality click on on-via charge?"... And I hate this question. The cause I hate it is because it assumes that the solution exists somewhere outside of your self even as it's certainly all very Glenda The Good Witch telling Dorothy "you've always had the energy, my expensive - you've had all of it alongside!"

While you could pay interest human beings talk about what a "correct" enterprise popular is, you already have your personal consequences which may be probably quite proper for in that you're proper now. That's the notable difficulty about any statistics gadgets you have were given got: everything that went into getting that stop result, which places you in a function to beautify the ones same consequences in a way someone else's "employer present day-day" in no way will.

We'll speak more approximately how to calculate what a very good click on-via charge is FOR YOU in Module four, but I'm glad to spoil the surprise with the aid of the usage of the use of telling you that in case you've sent electronic mail campaigns, it'll be a breeze on the way to discover the ideal solution and it lives to your private test paper.

Another focal aspect to start searching at is HOW your very very personal click on on-through costs fluctuate. For instance, your e-mail advertising service will provide you with the clicking-via rate for your massive marketing marketing campaign however I assignment you to look at how your superb tags and segments engage along facet your emails.

Let's re-use our example wherein your target marketplace are fitness specialists: it'd be valuable in an effort to continuously take a look at-in at the splendid degrees of engagement you're seeing from your fitness opposition, your private strolling shoes and your brand models/ambassadors.

Likewise, when you're walking a campaign this is heavy on the emails; it's a excellent idea to certainly peek in on how engaged your audience is inside the direction of the marketing advertising marketing campaign, and observe if there are variations with how click-happy one in all a kind segments or tags are, even inner one precise advertising marketing campaign.

There are numerous numbers you can have a look at and there are lots of things that unique people can let you understand approximately what's "specific" or what you must undertake as a "fashionable"; I say the grass is greener in which you water it and for all of the electricity you'll invest listening to others and evaluating yourself to consequences you don't have sufficient facts to even understand what it approach, you'd be higher off making an investment that identical strength taking your private information the greater mile.

Because, high quality, it could seem tedious to undergo each of your emails and have a look at your excellent segments, tags, challenge strains, and greater. But it's absolutely as tedious to pay attention to what others are saying you "should" do. You'll cross an entire lot further at the same time as you invest all that electricity into your very personal results than you can thru way of letting someone "should" on you. (Ew!)

HARD AND SOFT BOUNCE RATES

When you've got were given a study your internet internet page analytics, your bounce fee represents the folks that came for your web

web web page and left without delay, or in case you're a cool teenager, you may say they "bounced".

Because the vicinity is an unfair place, your leap fee technique some element absolutely special on the same time as we're speakme approximately your e-mail marketing analytics; your email leap rate approach your e mail could not be introduced to the e-mail cope with you sent it to and it consequently "bounced".

Since we've installation the sector as being an unfair location, permit's further complicate the problem due to the fact you have got two strategies for your emails to dance: with a "difficult" leap fee and with a "clean" bounce rate.

A tough leap manner the e-mail deal with you used is each invalid or you've got got been blocked from being able to ship emails to this address. When you deliver an email out of your inbox and without delay receive this type of creepy "mailer-daemon" replies, you're in hard soar territory.

A clean leap, as the decision indicates, is a extra transient trouble than its tough counterpart. There may additionally moreover have been a trouble with the e-mail server at the time you hit ship, the character's inbox may be too complete or possibly your electronic mail used too many huge photographs and GIFs and couldn't be introduced.

While I normally suggest for establishing your very own benchmarks for conversion charges and to no longer rely on organization necessities, there are exceptions to this rule and your leap price is taken into consideration one in every of them. (Other exceptions include your unsubscribe and unsolicited mail prices, which we'll talk approximately next.)

You in no way want each your clean bounce price or your difficult jump rate to be higher than 1% as this could have an effect to your giant deliverability, and we'll pass into a way to minimize your leap fee and beautify your e mail deliverability in Module 5.

UNSUBSCRIBE RATES

This one is quite self-explanatory: it's far the percentage of humans to whom you despatched emails that decided on to unsubscribe from your email list.

The greater people you ship emails to, the extra people you want to assume to unsubscribe. You don't need to be so concerned with the amount of individuals who unsubscribed however rather, you need to as an alternative reputation on the general percentage this represents from the list to which you sent it.

Your unsubscribe rate additionally shouldn't be seen as a terrible or horrible component and isn't always a mirrored photograph of techniques precious precise humans view your content. There are pretty a few reasons that people unsubscribe from e mail newsletters that don't have anything to do with the sender: they will be receiving "an excessive amount of" e mail everyday and they're doing an email purge, perhaps what you have got to mention and provide now not connects with wherein they may be in their own journey

, or perhaps they subscribed to your listing the usage of separate e-mail addresses and they will be cool with paying attention to from you sincerely once.

Unsubscribe fees aren't a metric to take in my view but having stated that, you do need to preserve your not unusual charge beneath 2%; if your unsubscribe rate is better than that, you likely produce other problems on hand (which we are capable of moreover address in Module 5) and you need to get some manage over those earlier than it affects your deliverability rate (which we can get into later on this module).

SPAM RATES

According to DataProt8, nearly 80 five% of all emails are junk mail, which interprets to a each day average of 122.33 billion e mail messages in line with day. As for the alternative 22.Forty three billion emails, that's the candy spot magnificence you need to be in. That's due to the truth unsolicited mail email is communication this is deemed as undesirable and solicited, and not simplest is it disturbing to gather but it may additionally be risky phishing or malware attempts designed to accumulate your statistics or take over your devices.

Depending at the location of the recipient to whom you are sending e mail, they may have regulation in area that protects them from those kinds of exploitative or junk emails, which we spoke about in the earlier section on criminal compliance in email advertising.

To avoid getting your emails categorized as junk mail or junk, your unsolicited mail rate need to be stored beneath 0.1%. This is a few other cause why you'll be OK with people unsubscribing out of your email list: you don't want to ship electronic mail to individuals who don't want them anyways as you'd alternatively have some human beings go away your listing than have all of your emails categorized as unsolicited mail.

This is likewise why you don't need your emails to be a system-gun of sales pitches; your deliverability WILL be impacted if you aren't offering the form of charge for your emails that humans need to and in reality do examine.

In fact, right here's a fun workout: test your e mail's junk folder right now. You in all likelihood have emails in there from human beings whose e mail listing you in reality did join as an awful lot as so why are they sitting within the junk folder? I'll allow you to draw your personal assumptions based totally on your personal studies, but I'd guess the person sending the ones emails has a bent to be excessive and heavy at the income pitches, and possibly doesn't provide loads of cost or a ordinary incentive to open their emails. This is some other cause why you need to be considerate of your e-mail method and ensure you're sending subjects that people in fact need to open, and not definitely sending what helps your bottom line.

OTHER EMAIL MARKETING METRICS

The above metrics can be furnished via the use of your email advertising and advertising and marketing issuer provider but there are other numbers that it doesn't offer and may be beneficial at the manner to maintain an eye fixed fixed on. However, those will every require that youto collect them some different region or which you'll need to calculate your self.

DELIVERABILITY RATES

Since we're close to unsolicited mail, allow's communicate approximately your deliverability expenses. To benefit notion to your deliverability, you'll ought to use an outdoor service to run an electronic mail deliverability check to gain your deliverability costs and have a examine what's known as your "sender reputation", at the manner to touch upon how your emails are being delivered to severa recipients (like Gmail, Outlook, and so on.). After all, step one to enhancing your electronic mail advertising outcomes is to make sure they're simply getting into the inboxes to which you're sending them in the first vicinity.

We'll stroll via this way, and advantage an data for what all of it method and what to search for in a later module, but I did need to mention it inside the metrics phase as a few component you'll want to understand as moving into the inbox is kinda-sorta-really a baseline requirement for strolling and optimizing electronic mail campaigns.

LIST GROWTH RATES

According to HubSpot9, your e mail list degrades with the useful resource of twenty-two.Five% every one year. This represents the general percentage of folks that unsubscribe or in any other case prevent organising and attractive along side your emails. You consequently continuously need to be aware about how your increase is taking location and also you additionally want to constantly artwork on growing your list to make up for those lost contacts.

By preserving tabs for your listing increase charge, you could make sure your listing growth is outpacing your list attrition. You can integrate this calculation into your quarterly assessment manner and to perform that, you'll want the following information factors for a particular term:

● Total variety of e-mail subscribers;

● Number of recent subscribers; and

• Number of unsubscribes.

You'll calculate (New subscribers) - (Unsubscribers), you then definately absolutely'll divide this via the general variety or people for your list, and in the long run multiply by means of the usage of the usage of 100.

I love examples so allow's make one out of this calculation: you've got an electronic mail list of two,000 people on the surrender of this place, and you brought 4 hundred of these this vicinity while 100 seventy five unsubscribed.

This manner 4 hundred -100 seventy five = 225 / 2000 = zero.One hundred twenty five x 100 = 12.5%.

This metric may be mainly precious even as tracking specific techniques you're the usage of. For instance, you may preserve your eye at the perfect list growth happening in conjunction with your classified ads/paid website traffic to keep on pinnacle of the tendencies with what you're spending versus what you're stepping into go back. After all, virtually due to the reality a person signed up on your email listing from an ad you ran doesn't suggest they stayed in your e mail listing or engaged beyond that initial self-discipline of signing up.

Likewise, in case you're going to recognition on listing growth previous to a launch, it's nicely to set some benchmarks and see how these numbers effect your not unusual launch general overall performance so you can use this data while you propose your next launch.

RESPONSE RATES

You in all likelihood won't have this metric on hand for your ordinary campaigns but there are instances in which you'll want to song what's called your response price. This is the proportion of folks who are actively attractive together collectively with your e mail with the resource of the usage of speaking a few factor lower lower back to you.

These are beneficial while you're sending out surveys or asking human beings for comments or opinions. You'll calculate this with the aid of manner of manner of taking the extensive form of human beings to whom you despatched the emails to divide it by means of way of the use of the quantity of individuals who replied in your emails, after which multiply with the useful resource of one hundred.

For instance, say you've got had been given an automatic collection designed to exit to human beings who've sold a particular product of yours and one of the emails in that collection includes a name-to-movement to offer a testimonial.

You obtained 20 testimonials remaining region from the 100 twenty five profits you made.

This method last vicinity's response fee on your product's testimonial requests come to be 16%, or 20 testimonials / one hundred twenty five income = zero.Sixteen x one hundred.

Again, you're not going to song the reaction charge for each unmarried e mail you ship out. You need to be specifically strategic approximately monitoring the ones because of the truth 1) these must be completed manually and a pair of) you need to have a cause for amassing this facts.

Some accurate motives can also include checking out specific scenario strains or calls-to-movement, switching out the order of your engagement-targeted e-mail delivery to peer if timing is a thing in whether or not or not humans are extra or a good deal a whole lot much less probably to have interaction with you, or perhaps to alternate the region of your options as buttons inside your email in place of redirecting them to a shape on your internet website. But it's critical to commonly preserve the save you motive in thoughts, this is which you need people to speak once more to you for a few particular cause, enter or feedback, and that's what we're measuring in this case.

SUBSCRIBER VALUE/REVENUE PER SUBSCRIBER

If you operate an all-in-one device that houses your earnings pages and cart processing like I do with Kartra, the platform itself will commonly provide you collectively with your e-mail subscriber charge. However, you could also calculate this for yourself if this isn't a statistics trouble this is provided for you along with your company.

Your subscriber fee can also be referred to as your "sales in step with subscriber" and it suggests what every subscriber is nicely well worth to you.

The cause this could be one of the most precious metrics a excellent manner to understand is whilst you're organized to spend money on areas like advertising and advertising and marketing; this will be what you use to forecast how a bargain you could control to pay for to spend to attract a lead further to to are expecting how an awful lot you can assume to make from each lead you enchantment to.

If your issuer doesn't robotically calculate this for you, you could calculate this thru the use of taking the sales you've generated thru your emails despatched over the last yr, and divide that through the amount of subscribers you have got.

Let's say you made $a hundred,000 in income and you've were given a list of 5,000 people.

This technique that each of your e mail subscribers is definitely without a doubt worth $20/twelve months to you.

Start with an annual baseline as your benchmark and then depending at the frequency of your critiques, combine this calculation as a ordinary part of your monthly or quarterly "health tests". You'll need to maintain seeing this extensive variety on an annual basis as some quarters are extra release- and profits-targeted than others; you can assume to look a trustworthy quantity of variance primarily based on how and what you had been advertising and marketing and advertising and marketing in some unspecified time in the future of that location however searching at the annual big image probable offers you a more balanced, massive examine of your subscriber price.

This is each one-of-a-kind motive why it's a super concept to tag how people opted into your email list and moreover ruin down the price of your subscribers based on wherein they came from. This way, while you're making prepared to invest into a specific method, you've got were given an idea of what the price of those varieties of subscribers are as compared to others.

CONVERSION RATES

Last but absolutely no longer least, we've got to speak about your e mail conversion costs. Now, I really have a few strong thoughts and feelings about how humans speak approximately their conversion costs, and I delve into the troubles I surely have with "precise humans's conversion quotes" in my e-book on publishing, monitoring and improving your traditional digital advertising and marketing campaigns and strategies referred to as Results On Repeat.

But even as someone says some thing like, "My release transformed at 20%"... I'm over right right here asking, "converted what to twenty% of what, exactly?"

Because to calculate a conversion price, you need a beginning and an prevent. If we stay with the instance of a release, you can convert 20% of your e-mail listing to income to your release, but you may additionally convert 20% of your e-mail to visits of your launch sales internet internet web page... and people may be very tremendous memories being cautioned. (And your accountant simply is of the equal opinion with me!)

I may want to even venture to mention that "e-mail list" isn't normally a particular enough location to begin; ultimately, you have got maximum of these segments and tags for your email list and you can count on to see a completely unique conversion to sales out of your modern e-mail list than you can see from the a bargain-warmer part of those who have been at the waitlist on your next launch.

This is why I'm generally suspicious of using vague, undefined conversion prices in different human beings's advertising and marketing, and it's why I inspire you to interest for your private test paper. When you're searching at your personal specific numbers, based mostly on your personal subscribers whose interest and alternatives you're clean approximately, you're capable of understand WHAT your conversion expenses recommend, what they're telling you about the regions for optimization and also you get to outline success on your very personal phrases and numbers, actually.

But returned to the numbers: as we've set up, you need a starting and an surrender so that you can calculate a conversion fee and that's due to the fact you divide the forestall end end result through in that you started out out from, and then multiply with the useful resource of one hundred.

Let's roll out an instance and say you need to calculate the conversion rate for email subscribers to income net page visits. You made 50 sales (your give up give up result) from the 2000 email subscribers you despatched that promotional e-mail to (your location to start).

This manner your e mail listing had a conversion charge = 50 income / 2000 electronic mail subscribers = zero.Zero.Five x a hundred = 2.Five% conversion charge from e-mail subscribers to earnings.

Meanwhile, you had 4 hundred humans for your e mail listing who confirmed interest on this offer earlier than you launched it, either through asking to be on a waitlist or via the use of signing up for a associated mission or workshop you supplied. This way your conversion price for those heat subscribers to your electronic mail list transformed to earnings at 12.Five% because 50 profits / 4 hundred human beings = 0.One hundred twenty five x one hundred = 12.Five%.

Why is it useful to interrupt it down like this? Because whilst you recognise a portion of your subscribers will convert 10% better than some different, you may find out precisely how precious and the manner profitable it'd be to increase how lots of your email subscribers are in that segment of your email list preceding to launching.

It may be profitable to push your launch out via one week to get more human beings to take part in the challenge or workshop that warmed this section up so effectively, and you could combine this warming cycle as a part of your next release.

Collecting and reading data is in no way about the numbers themselves; it's approximately the tremendous mind and insights you carry to them.

To examine greater on conversion price optimization throughout all of your ordinary virtual advertising and marketing techniques, visit e-book.Omgrowth.Com/e mail and check out the hyperlink to my flagship e-book on the priority called Results On Repeat.

A WORD ABOUT EMAIL LINK SHARING

Always try and direct your electronic mail site visitors to a net website online which you very non-public.

Why?

Because there's continually that one teen who takes it too some distance and ruins it for the rest folks, electronic mail web hosting and delivery services aren't obsessed with emails that share hyperlinks for things like Amazon products.

When you include Amazon links to your emails, you hazard impacting your sender recognition and email your deliverability.

So what's an Amazon companion to do?

I suggest you create a separate net web page or web website on line wherein you direct your e-mail subscribers to in which you may feature and link to the ones Amazon merchandise you promote. If you want an example of what this may appear like, visit omgrowthbooks.Com to look wherein I ship all of my e-mail visitors after I'm promoting certainly one of my books.

There are some delivered blessings to taking some of the ones precautions that is going beyond trying no longer to dissatisfied the e-mail gods; while you are making a addiction of usually directing website online traffic to a touchdown net page or net site which you very own, tune and control, it method you're higher positioned to view and understand your normal performance traits, even on the same time as you're promoting gives and belongings which you don't necessarily personal.

YOUR EMAIL TRACKING SYSTEM

Before we get began with HOW you're going to location intentional, data-pushed monitoring in vicinity in your email marketing and advertising usual overall performance, I need to remind you that if you want to see what people are doing on your internet site after they click on on-thru out of your emails, you want to have internet site analytics monitoring your internet internet page common overall overall performance.

As such, I am working beneath the perception that you have analytics software program application established for your website.

If you want assist with this, I bypass extra in-depth about this in my ebook Results On Repeat which you could find out at e-book.Omgrowth.Com/e-mail   and   I communicate about this on episode fifty three and fifty 4 of the OMGrowth Podcast.

The monitoring system we're putting in area here will display up within the ones internet site analytics evaluations. If you take a look at your internet site analytics right now, you'll see that your e mail advertising and marketing provider likely does placed some tracking in area however it's a chunk "meh" and loads of messy. The inconsistency and absence of clarity doesn't do you any favors close to honing in for your normal overall performance for whatever, a whole lot plenty lots less your site site visitors coming mainly from email.

But with my easy and clear tracking device, you could placed a prevent to all that cluttered reporting and as an alternative, generate reporting that appears greater like this one from Fathom Analytics:

Isn't this easy at the eyes? Here, we are able to short see that our email promotions are out-pacing all of the specific campaigns blended but that we're no matter the fact that obtaining greater interest from our social media fanatics than we are from our advertisements or our referral website visitors.

If you depend upon the default monitoring that other systems automatically generate on your behalf, you could have information however you'll in no manner have smooth opinions like this that you may use to make snappy, records-pushed alternatives. Meanwhile, my naming convention is designed to now not handiest provide you with smooth-to-take a look at reviews like this, but it also positions your gives the front-and-center in which they belong so you can without trouble clear out your marketing efforts based totally surely at the particular gives you want to sell.

After all, at the same time as you're looking at your numbers, you commonly want in case you want to answer the quite easy question: "WHAT WAS THIS PROMOTION FOR? WHAT WERE MY EFFORTS MEANT TO PROMOTE?"

Whether you're sending an e mail, whether or now not you're presenting a discount in your podcast listeners, whether or no longer you're taking component with someone else, whether or not you're posting to social media - you're selling each considered one in each of your paid gives or surely one in every of your loose gives.

Let's study every exclusive instance and this time, we'll take a look at a Plausible Analytics document at the general performance of a specific advertising method, like the emails in an evergreen profits series:

By getting intentional approximately the way you're tracking the links within the automatic emails you're sending, you may see that the number one email is attracting the most site visitors - it is regular - but there's a few factor approximately that 4th electronic mail that is bringing more of those e-mail subscribers on your income net page than the second or third emails are. This is definitely an possibility to dig a touch deeper and discover what it's miles approximately that 4th e mail that is connecting so nicely and to see if you can convey greater of a few thing this is into the other emails.

With this tracking tool, you may take a zoomed out view to look how your e-mail advertising and advertising and advertising and marketing compares to specific advertising and marketing efforts, and you could zoom in to look how specific emails, kinds of email campaigns (i.E. Launches vs evergreen sequences) or maybe precise kinds of hyperlinks (i.E. Button vs text vs video vs snap shots) carry out on your severa campaigns.

To do that, we're going to use what are called Urchin Tracking Modules, or what the cool children like us will speak over with as UTMs. These are little snippets of code at the manner to be brought to the surrender of any link you are emailing.

Any UTM parameter you upload will constantly override some component monitoring is already there and whilst used efficaciously, that's a outstanding difficulty.

This technique which you're overriding "their manner" of reporting on your site visitors at the side of your very personal approach of reporting - a totally "boss" detail to do, through the use of the way - this will bring about more regular, actionable reporting for you. Well performed!

You will need 1 detail and 3 important parameters to music your advertising and marketing campaign.

The detail you want is a LINK to which you may be directing your traffic. You're already sharing links on your emails so this likely isn't a addiction you want to growth or located hundreds perception into.

You will, but, ought to get inside the addiction of taking into account your three essential parameters and right right here's the TL;DR on what they constitute:

• CAMPAIGN = this may define WHAT you are promoting;

• MEDIUM = this will outline HOW you're promoting your provide; and

• SOURCE = this could define WHERE you're selling.

Your CAMPAIGN parameter can be tagged as follows: "utm_campaign=".

This permits you to area your offers because the centerpiece of everything you're promoting. This makes it possible as a way to assess all the techniques you're selling your gives, like this:

You may additionally even should encompass a MEDIUM parameter identified as "&utm_medium=" and a SOURCE parameter recognized as "&utm_source=". These are related however unique.

Your MEDIUM is the type of communique you're the use of to sell your provide, and because this e-book is focused on e mail marketing, you're right if you guessed that most of the examples on this e-book will use "email" as its MEDIUM. Meanwhile, your SOURCE will further outline and offer specifics as to the manner you're using that medium. For instance, you may turn out to be aware of the deliver of these emails as "newsletters" or "pronounces" while you can have an automated profits series you name "evergreen" or "funnel".

The mixture of those parameters will will will let you differentiate the results you're getting primarily based totally at the types of promotions you're sending.

Here's a bit picture breakdown to higher visualize what each parameter is meant to symbolize:

I'm a huge fan of examples so allow's use one:

Let's say the income web page to your club lives at https://salespage.Com and you're sending a single e mail reminding your list that they can be part of your club.

This way your CAMPAIGN is your "club", your MEDIUM is "e mail" and your SOURCE is "broadcast".

The link you percent will appear to be this: https://salespage.Com?Utm_campaign=membe rship&utm_medium=electronic mail&utm_source=broadcast

Meanwhile, your analytics platform will see and accumulate plenty of those insights and history statistics you've precise approximately the character of the links even as you percent them in this manner. This records is probably categorized on your opinions because of this.

#PROTIP

Don't use regions or capital letters with UTM parameters.

If you have were given a CAMPAIGN you need to name "Signature Offer", you may either need to apply a sprint ("signature-offer"), an acronym or abbreviation ("sigoff") or make all of it one word ("signatureoffer").

The key right here is to set up a naming convention for each provide and to stick to it like your outcomes depend upon it… because they do!

After all, your reporting will simplest be as everyday as you are with the use of the same naming convention for your gives.

You also can wonder if it subjects what order you placed your parameters in and the answer is not any. It makes no difference what order you located your parameters in; you may area your CAMPAIGN parameter earlier than your MEDIUM parameter one time, and you may position your SOURCE parameter first yet again and it acquired't depend which order they may be in at any time. Your analytics software program program will accumulate all the data regardless of the manner you function it.

What DOES rely, despite the fact that, is which you embody your LINK on the facet of your 3 crucial parameters: CAMPAIGN, MEDIUM and SOURCE.

But what approximately non-essential parameters?

Sticking with the above example, we are capable of similarly outline that this hyperlink have become in an email despatched on November 30, 2023 by way of way of manner of inclusive of an non-obligatory CONTENT parameter that might appearance something like "&utm_content=20231130" and this can tag the traveller to the date on which your email turned into despatched.

If you need to get "next degree" approximately your monitoring, you may furthermore use the TERM parameter that will help you differentiate what type of content fabric material that link have become clicked from. For example, you can have video links, photograph links and textual content links for your email, and you want to assess how every of these carry out for you. In this example, you can upload TERM parameters that would appear to be "&utm_term=vid", "&utm_term=img" and "&utm_term=txt", respectively.

Let's take a look at this hyperlink: https://salespage.Com?Utm_term=vid&utm_medium=e-mail&utm_content=20231130&utm_source=broadcast&utm_campaign=membership

You can see that this hyperlink is set up to tune 6 essential factors of our promotional efforts. Namely, it'll track the engagement of those who clicked through 1) to the profits internet web page 2) from the video link three) we embedded in the email 4) that become sent on

November 30, 2023 5) to reminding our gift/elegant subscribers of 6) the club we must offer.

The delivered advantage to getting more unique with using CONTENT and TERM parameters is you could isolate the ones in your common reviews and also you're then capable of see, for example, how embedded motion pictures carry out for you as an average advertising method rather than embedded pictures or text links.

ABOUT "CONTENT" & "TERM" PARAMETERS IN GA4

If you are the use of Google Analytics as your analytics software program software program, the most recent model of Google Analytics called GA4 has modified CONTENT and TERM with one single new parameter called ID, which seems like "&utm_id=" and you will should modify and restriction your use of UTMs therefore.

Know that Google Analytics is not your handiest alternative for analytics software software and in my view, it is not your great alternative each.

Google Analytics isn't privacy-compliant software proper out-of-the-area; you will need to alter some of your settings and embed some of custom coding to make Google Analytics legally compliant to crook suggestions like GDPR (and if you want to pay attention more approximately why I don't forget the platform to be a elaborate desire for masses of solopreneurs and small commercial business enterprise owners, be aware of episode fifty three of the OMGrowth Podcast.)

Instead, I advise Fathom Analytics or Plausible Analytics (and I speak approximately the variations among them and why you may select out one over the opportunity on episode fifty 4 of the OMGrowth Podcast) and I'm thrilled to document that each systems will document the CONTENT and TERM parameters said on this ebook.

They also are the systems I use to offer any of the reporting examples I use throughout this e-book.

Any time you're dubious as to how a UTM parameter will seem on your critiques, open a "actual-time report" and enter your tagged link in a browser to check and see how your parameters are being recorded with the beneficial useful resource of your analytics software program software program of preference.

If you're feeling a bit itchy approximately all of this and questioning, "But Lanie, I'm in no manner going to take into account all of this"... Amazing! I'm glad to pay attention it and I might also hate a very good manner to waste too much of your progressive genius in this count.

Your mind space is lots higher used on springing up with extremely good advertising strategies and messages, and this isn't some thing you need to memorize or you may ever be anticipated to generate from the pinnacle of your head.

I virtually want you to understand HOW they art work and WHY they artwork this manner because of the reality I set the following module as a whole lot as be just like we're once more in college; you'll be capable of reproduction my check paper and get an A with all the codes and hyperlinks already written out for you as they relate in your precise techniques.

Chapter 3: The Anatomy Of Your Email Campaigns

Even with a few issue as specific as e mail marketing and marketing, there are such loads of more techniques and campaigns that fall within that one manner you could promote yourself, your gives and your content.

This is why I need to take a 2nd earlier than we dive into all the functionality email campaigns you can be sending to remind you that just because of the truth some aspect is indexed right here, it does now not mean you have to or which you need to appoint every of the campaigns listed right right here. These strategies aren't supposed to be a checklist of e-mail advertising and advertising techniques to combine into your operations; instead, have a have a look at them as an define of the alternatives to be had in order to hire.

Furthermore, that may be a e-book approximately tracking and improving your electronic mail advertising and advertising and marketing efforts, however display yourself some grace and realize that you'll in no way be able to improve all your campaigns, .

Your first-rate wager for reaching Email Marketing Optimization is to restrict your reputation to enhancing simply one crucial electronic mail advertising and marketing and marketing and advertising approach at a time.

While you will be enhancing one area at a time, your tracking DOES need to be mounted region earlier than you hit "ship" or "time desk" on a few trouble. After all, information is not retroactive, and as quick as your electronic mail is added to those inboxes, there's no manner of going over again to put the tracking in place which you'll need on the way to improve your email effects.

This is why I emphasize the significance of putting your tracking in place with every and each broadcast you ship shifting in advance, and to put in force the tracking into your sequences as quickly as feasible.

And look, I'm making this goofy-diploma-smooth if you want to do. When it involves mapping out any form of method, I take the "mapping" element literally by using the use of the usage of developing a manner map that you can with out issue visualize.

That's why I've designed this module to define:

1. The smooth assets implemented in each advertising and advertising approach;

2. The actual matters you will want to track and the manner you could track them; and

three. A manner map so you can visualize the strategy.

In the last module, we went via HOW monitoring your campaigns works, but this module will spell out the coding template for each extraordinary approach.

If you need to down load and/or print the workflows from this section, visit e-book.Omgrowth.Com/e mail to get them bundled in a on hand PDF for smooth future reference.

Just as this module isn't a tick list, the ones campaigns aren't exhaustive, both. If some element is not indexed right right here, that doesn't suggest it isn't a valid technique. There will constantly be a ultra-modern-day strategy, a contemporary promotional method, a cutting-edge spin-off to the triumphing campaigns we're the use of. Let's additionally not forget about about approximately that creative marketers like your self are continuously developing with innovative methods to promote themselves on this ever-evolving employer. This is why I emphasize your records of HOW tracking works because of the reality after you "get" that, you'll be capable of music any technique you provide you with.

If there's an electronic mail advertising and marketing method you need to tune that isn't indexed proper here, remember which one it most carefully resembles and use that as your guide or template.

We're going initially broadcasts and an appropriate kinds of unmarried emails you normally time table or ship.

BROADCASTS

Any e mail that you time desk or ship is what we're capable of be regarding as a "broadcast" but there are masses of unique techniques that those one-off emails are sent to assist. We'll walk through each of the number one ones however look at that counting on the email marketing and marketing company company you use, your platform might also additionally additionally check with those as "pronounces", "

newsletters" or in all likelihood even "campaigns".

You, on the other hand, are welcome to name the ones one-off emails you're sending with any name you pick out out, which embody giving them abbreviated little acronyms like "bc" for broadcast, "nl" for e-publication or "oo" for one-off. While I will direct you want air website visitors control as to whilst you need to replace it up based totally on specific outcomes you'll need to hone in on, we are able to use "broadcast" for our abilties of identifying single emails we're sending right here on out.

The key to having an powerful naming convention and clean reporting is to be consistent with a few component you pick out.

We apprehend the MEDIUM is "e-mail", we set up that we can discover the SOURCE as "broadcast" and subsequent, we'll outline the CONTENT to clarify WHICH one-off e mail we sent. I like to use the date you sent the e-mail (YYYYMMDD) but I've visible human beings choose to use key terms or difficulty strains in an effort to advantage on the spot insights as to what the content material fabric of the e-mail modified into.

You also can use the TERM parameter in your key phrases or trouble lines for further clarification as properly. The preference is yours as to the way you want to put together this however all another time, the maximum vital component is that you be steady with enforcing a few factor choice you do make.

This way your one-off e mail campaigns/famous or random broadcasts may be installed as follows:

- CAMPAIGN = call of your offer;

- MEDIUM = electronic mail;

- SOURCE = broadcast;

- CONTENT = date/key-word/concern.

And it might be built like this:

https://www.Hyperlink.Com?Utm_campaign=product&utm_source=broadcast&utm_medium=e-mail&utm_content=20231231

Which would possibly assist you to see and examine how all of your one-off emails selling that particular product finished, like so:

This manner, you can without difficulty hone in on how your random email reminders approximately that one provide are acting. Consider this sort of tagging absolutely the baseline for any email campaigns you're sending out moving in advance.

But what about on the equal time because the emails you're sending otherwise you're scheduling which can be a piece greater intentional, and are a part of a larger attempt?

Let's discover those.

LIVE PROMOTIONS - LAUNCHING AND FLASH SALES

When you are launching a digital products or services, you're focusing your strive on getting more website online site visitors to that earnings net page during a specific time period (or what's referred to as your "launch period"), usually through targeted on your gift fans and the email listing subscribers you've been constructing a courting with.

The consequences you'll see from this advertising and marketing and marketing approach need to be specific from while you're casually promoting the identical offer. As a data-driven virtual marketer, you'll want to recognize how your specific styles of electronic mail campaigns carry out for the identical provide. For instance, what outcomes are you seeing out of your reminder emails in preference to live promotions in region of your automation sequences?

That's why you want to deliberately tag the hyperlinks you're sharing sooner or later of your stay vending to music how this specific approach is appearing for you inside the context of the entirety else you will be doing. After all, you're typically firing off greater emails inside the course of a release length - and also you frequently have more than one considered one of a type portions going out in keeping with day - and there's a whole lot of notion to advantage and movement you could take even as you apprehend how they every carry out.

Examples assist, proper? Let's say you want to recognize which emails were your great performers, each in terms of driving website online traffic in addition to creating profits. By the use of an intentional tracking device in some unspecified time in the future of our launch, this Plausible Analytics record suggests us that notwithstanding the fact that e mail #1 introduced us the maximum website site visitors…

…it have become email #4 that generated the maximum income:

While it is not unusual to your in advance emails to get higher open costs and for your emails closest to the give up of your promotional length to get the maximum sales, you'll need to investigate what it become about e mail #1 and #4 that changed into so appealing to look how you may examine your findings through future promotions or sequences. You'll additionally want to pay near interest to what occurred in electronic mail #3 that made it this kind of low-performer in evaluation on your specific efforts and observe what insights and takeaways you examine right right here, too.

In this case, I may want to want to apprehend what made e mail #four and #2 so treasured? What happened in e mail #3 that it modified into your least worthwhile and least attractive electronic mail thru this form of massive margin? Why did you've got got were given loads hobby generated with email #1 and yet it lacked within the follow-thru?

Look at your situation strains similarly to the number one line of text that indicates up within the inbox and dissect the language and location on your calls-to-motion that made people so click on on on-happy at the top appearing emails versus the alternative emails.

It may be your timing, it could be the usage of countdown timers or the situation lines or the calls-to-motion - you will have a look at the content cloth of your top performer however you could additionally study how it is exquisite from the opportunity emails, which includes individuals who did NOT perform properly as this info can be clearly as treasured in an effort to realise and recognize.

To get data like this, regardless of the truth that, you'll use your UTM parameters as follows to your release period:

● CAMPAIGN = name of your offer;

● MEDIUM = e mail;

● SOURCE = some element along the lines of "promo" or "release";

● CONTENT = you can use the "order" + "date" approach that will help you understand which e-mail within the collection this link changed into embedded in (order) and even as it changed into despatched (date);

● TERM = an non-compulsory field you could use to detail which specific advertising you're monitoring. (i.E. "&utm_term=black-friday-2023")

Here's a workflow for the manner you would set those emails up:

While I said consistency have come to be key collectively together with your naming convention - and it is! - we are intentional approximately how we are converting the SOURCE parameter proper here from "broadcast" to "promo".

After all, we need our critiques to clearly display the distinction the various income web page visits and earnings we crafted from random emails we despatched promoting our product (which we named "broadcast"), as well as the live promotions like we're speakme about in this example of a launch (named "promo") and later we can visit the automated profits sequences we might also furthermore have in place (which we are capable of pick out out as "evergreen").

Our purpose right here is to use the SOURCE parameter in a way that works to our gain and makes our reporting as smooth as possible as to what the advertising and marketing advertising marketing campaign motive modified into.

For instance, permit's say that within the direction of the one year, you have got got big launches but you moreover mght have much less extensive flash income. You may pick out out to find out your SOURCE as "&utm_source=promo" to your launches and then use "&utm_source=flash" on your flash income.

By doing this, you're giving yourself the superpower of being capable of clear out the consequences of your modern-day stay promoting in competition to the final one you did, and you're able to examine the performance of severa styles of promotions in competition to each different.

LIVE EVENTS - WEBINARS AND EMAIL CHALLENGES

There are lots of super methods to combine stay sports that promote your services or products. You can host an event as a lead-up in your launch, you may run it as its personal provide, or you may even host joint project collaborations to art work with someone who has a similar target market to yours and get in the front of each awesome's people.

Live sports are a hint awesome from live promotions within the revel in that we're commonly looking at a segment of your target marketplace who've already made a micro-commitment to you. While you're pitching a suggestion to this segment, they're already "bought" on some thing you're speakme approximately due to the reality they've opted in and feature intentionally agreed to accumulate an inflow of emails approximately the content material cloth you're sharing.

I is probably the use of the time period "webinar" as being interchangeable with any live event we're promoting and internet internet hosting however you can pick out out or be used to special terminology, like workshops, sports, tutorials, education or seminars.

What we're talking approximately on this phase is any form of event where you're offering a right, packaged reading experience wherein a person raised their hand and said, "positive! I need to research this from you." This moreover manner we're speakme about a warm target marketplace you're getting the possibility to further have interaction.

The anatomy of a stay occasion will ruin down into 2 sections:

1. Promoting the stay event/webinar that people be a part of up to; and

2. Tracking the placed up-event income overall performance for the offer you're promoting or pitching following the live occasion/webinar.

Let's start by using way of manner of mapping out that big photo view, we ought to?

Since the start is always an awesome region to begin, allow's damage down the number one segment of this method.

YOUR LIVE EVENT PROMOTION

The first a part of this advertising campaign is to signal people up to your stay event and to perform that, you may sell the stay occasion in all of the usual locations which you promote yourself and your gives.

Because we're focusing on email, the campaigns you're sharing on this example to sell signal-u.S.A.To your webinar out of your subscribers will appear to be this:

The emails you deliver out could be broken down as follows:

• CAMPAIGN = webinar find out or acronym;

• MEDIUM = e mail;

• SOURCE = a few element along the traces of "promo";

• CONTENT = you could use the "order" + "date" components to help you find out which e mail within the collection this link changed into embedded in (order) and even as it modified into despatched (date).

There are one-of-a-type methods you'll promote your live occasion than clearly for your email subscribers, of direction. For instance, your Instagram bio link can be switched out to look like this:

- CAMPAIGN = webinar title or acronym;

- MEDIUM = social;

- SOURCE = instagram;

- CONTENT = bio

While this book is all approximately email advertising and advertising, I did need to at least contact on and convey some interest to the fact that every hyperlink you percent to sell any offer is some thing you may need to attach comparable tracking to.

For greater at the manner to tune all of the methods in which you sell your gives, go to e-book.Omgrowth.Com/electronic mail to test out Results On Repeat, my book on publishing, tracking and enhancing your normal digital advertising efforts.

FOR WEBINARS: Once human beings are signed up for your webinar, you'll commonly ship them an email confirming that they'll be signed up for the webinar and you'll additionally have a series of emails going out right earlier than the event at the way to have all the links they need to wait the actual webinar.

The collection of emails that go out among signing up for the webinar and the webinar itself don't need to be tracked or tagged.

You CAN track them if you have a protracted sign-up period and also you want to see how engaged human beings are and stay during that during-amongst time of signing up and on the same time as you go live, but you normally aren't linking to 3 element in the ones emails so there wouldn't be some thing to song.

If you do determine to proportion hyperlinks which you need to music at this section, ensure you absolutely endorse alongside aspect your SOURCE parameter that those are the in-between emails meant to hold up engagement, and they may be not real event emails meant for conversions.

After all, that's usually the "save you undertaking" for live activities: you're losing all this information for gratis with the goal of changing to income, that's what we're doing and tracking within the next segment.

YOUR POST-EVENT SALES PERFORMANCE

Your live occasion normally serves to at the least one) display off your knowledge and know-how, at the same time as 2) supply a "short win" that is a mini-model of the wins they'll expect out of your paid offer.

With a webinar, that brief win is framed at the prevent of the stay occasion as an opportunity to keep those wins coming with the acquisition of your offer. You then deliver take a look at-up emails reminding your webinar attendees of the reasons why they want to preserve the ones wins going, and their engagement with the ones reminder emails is what we're going to song next.

(An e mail task is installation a touch otherwise from a webinar but we must begin someplace so we're diving into the webinar first.)

Once they've visible your webinar, you may direct your webinar attendees from the education to a profits web page. That hyperlink may be tagged like you see in this top segment:

I inspire you to limit how prolonged you keep your replay up. After all, the goal isn't to provide the live webinar in perpetuity (but there may be a time and region for that approach, which we'll cover inside the Recorded/Repurposed "Live" Event section growing).

Remember that your goal with this training is to introduce the benefits of what your paid offer can produce and to convert that show off of your facts to earnings. Once your target market has had a risk to look at your schooling, you need to direct your web page visitors to the profits web page and you want to be steady collectively with your messaging as to what the following step is to take after your schooling.

The greater barriers and obstacles you region spherical your replay period, the clearer your reviews can be with figuring out conversions from the training instead of the observe-up emails you'll be sending. You also can anticipate to look better conversion charges to income because of the reality those subscribers will constantly be seeing the profits net page for buy in choice on your schooling.

Your put up-webinar e mail collection may additionally have parameters that appear to be this:

● CAMPAIGN = name of your offer;

● MEDIUM = email;

● SOURCE = a few aspect alongside the traces of "positioned up-webinar" or "webinar-observe-up";

● CONTENT = define which e mail inside the collection we're speaking about (i.E. Email #1 vs e-mail #5, as established inside the method map).

● TERM = if this is a webinar you run regularly, you could use this parameter to define which advertising and marketing period this modified into. (i.E. &utm_term=summer2023)

This will allow you to understand which email converted the high-quality, which one converted the worst, and what the engagement end up for every of them. After all, there may be one email that noticed the satisfactory click on on-through fee however the one with a lower click on on-via charge is wherein your profits had been extraordinary transformed. This is records you want to apprehend to get higher outcomes collectively with your subsequent webinar, and advantage belief as to how your live webinar profits carry out in evaluation to the earnings you're making from your replays and your have a look at-up emails.

On the opportunity hand, an email challenge has a few versions with how you may track your results.

Instead of turning in that short win in a single session, you're turning in micro-wins for your subscribers at some point of more than one emails (generally three-5). Only after you've gained a few footing on your task do you start pitching your paid offer via however some other series of emails. There are some instances where you could sell your paid provide midway via and at the element of the actual electronic mail project itself as well.

I've laid this workflow out to expose you methods you will code each e mail if you had been, in truth, starting to sell your paid provide in electronic mail #three, whilst the venture remains occurring.

Your e-mail project would possibly map out to look some element like this:

It's an entire lot of e-mail and this is all of the greater purpose to intentionally tag those links and better understand how the overall go along with the go with the flow of every e-mail is appearing.

● Where are human beings dropping off for your undertaking?

● How engaged in some unspecified time in the future of the undertaking are folks that transformed? Which inclinations do you need to study and capitalize on?

- What and in which are your possibilities to increase engagement?

A little #protip for better monitoring your email challenges is to preserve the real content material cloth of your email as quick as feasible, and stress your subscribers to click on on through to an internet net web page wherein they may get proper of access to the whole thing they need for that day's venture. Set your emails up to be cliffhangers that strain your readers to engage collectively together with your content material cloth.

Not only do the ones click on-throughs and engagement decorate your sender popularity, but it moreover permits you to look in greater element how extended they're attractive with that day's substances, how masses of your movies they're viewing, how many virtual downloads they're making. You can more with out issues emerge as aware about the types of materials and content material your aim market responds first rate to, and that is records you may parlay into the manner you're selling everything else you want to offer.

Your electronic mail task series can have hyperlinks with parameters that appear to be this:

• CAMPAIGN = your challenge name;

• This will no longer be your offer because of the fact in some unspecified time inside the future of the venture, we're certainly selling engagement within the project so the project itself is the provide at this factor. When you're sending your emails selling the offer you'll be pitching afterwards or at the same time as you encompass hyperlinks that direct readers to the offer you're the use of this challenge to promote, those emails can also additionally have the CAMPAIGN parameter due to the fact the provide (see below).

• MEDIUM = e mail;

• SOURCE = challenge;

• CONTENT = define which email inside the collection we're talking approximately (i.E. Electronic mail #1 vs e mail #5, as proven in the technique map).

Any emails sent put up-venture or hyperlinks you're embedding in the route of the challenge which might be designed to direct site site visitors for your paid offer must have parameters that appear to be this:

- CAMPAIGN = name of your provide;

- MEDIUM = e mail;

- SOURCE = challenge;

- CONTENT = define which electronic mail in the collection we're speakme about (i.E. E-mail #1 vs email #5, as proven in the technique map).

Keep in mind that in case you ARE selling your paid provide within the course of the actual e-mail task, then you can have unique kinds of parameters in the identical emails: one will direct humans to the mission content fabric even as the opportunity will direct human beings to the paid offer. As established in the closing approach map, you will want to replace your CAMPAIGN parameter to nicely apprehend what unique provide you embedded each hyperlink to promote.

JOINT VENTURE LIVE EVENTS

While collaborations and joint ventures are their personal situation completely, I is probably remiss now not to say it right here as they're a well-known manner of the usage of live activities and your emails are simply a trouble in promoting them.

After all, participating with others is a notable way to grow your non-public electronic mail listing via stepping into the front of audiences who are just like yours.

If we take the webinar workflow, your "Post-Event Sales Performance" part of the monitoring will stay the identical.

However, you'll need to change your "Live Event Promotion" tracking in which you're using humans to sign up for up. You'll need to ask your collaboration associate to use the hyperlinks as you've coded them, so you may be as follows:

• CAMPAIGN = webinar perceive or acronym;

- MEDIUM = electronic mail;

- SOURCE = a few detail like "collab", "joint-undertaking" or even "jv";

- CONTENT = you could use the "order" + "date" method that will help you understand which e mail inside the collection this link emerge as embedded in (order) or even as it modified into sent (date).

I can also pay unique interest to tagging them as referred through your collaborator in your personal reference and standard performance tracking functions.

For greater on monitoring your joint venture efforts with collaborations, buddies and traveller speaking possibilities like summits and podcasts, go to ebook.Omgrowth.Com/e-mail to discover my ebook dedicated to tracking those specific advertising and advertising techniques.

RECORDED/REPURPOSED "LIVE" EVENTS

There comes a element with an entire lot of webinars where you've finished your awesome sauce presentation so normally and you stick the touchdown so often that you have the dreamy conversion expenses to reveal it. You also can decide to take a recording of that webinar and repurpose your presentation into an select-in that allows you to then sell your offer on vehicle-pilot; essentially, you want to do precisely what you likely did at the stay webinar... minus the stay detail.

Your monitoring for this will be exactly similar to if you're going live, besides in location of your emails being scheduled, they'll as a substitute be a part of a chain, like this:

FEEDBACK AND SURVEYS

You most genuinely can and are welcome to complicate the monitoring of your remarks and surveys by means of tagging those links with parameters. In reality, in case you're sending masses of specific segments to at least one single remarks form or survey, it is able to be really worth seeing how engaged your remarkable segments are and how their feedback differs .

However, if we're talking approximately feedback and surveys which are, say, a testimonial for your provide, you don't need to tag your links to recognize how they reached this form; sincerely, they supplied your offer and that's how they found and clicked this hyperlink. If you need some statistics as to how engaged your consumers are in presenting you with feedback, you can revisit the segment on RESPONSE RATES in Module 2 but you'll basically have a observe how many customers you had and how many humans submitted the favored feedback.

Having said that, you may want to evaluate whether your clients are extra engaged with the examine-up emails asking for comments as opposed to the link in the real content material material of the offer. In this example, the parameters to your comments request emails can look some issue like this:

• CAMPAIGN = offername-remarks;

• MEDIUM = e-mail;

- SOURCE = feedback.

Meanwhile, the links you embed to your course or provide need to look like this:

- CAMPAIGN = offername-comments;

- MEDIUM = offername;

- SOURCE = embedded-hyperlink.

Note that in this case, the CAMPAIGN parameter isn't your provide because of the fact we are reserving your CAMPAIGN parameter for the methods in which we are selling our offers. In this situation, we're not promoting the provide however instead, we're selling feedback on a proposal that has already transformed to a sale and we don't need our reporting for the ones very different things to be blended.

But this is a great example an remarkable manner to appearance that there are instances while you could not need monitoring in location, and it absolutely emphasizes the importance of asking yourself "WHAT am I trying to sell here and in which are my possibilities to enhance the way I'm promoting this issue?"

If there aren't any possibilities for development or if it doesn't assist an offer you're linking to and marketing and advertising and marketing, then there may be no need to tune those results.

SEQUENCES

I touched in this inside the introduction because of the truth I didn't want you to pay interest it for the number one time at this midway point within the e-book, however almost about monitoring your electronic mail advertising and marketing typical performance, the excellent vicinity to begin is along with your sequences. Your e-mail advertising and marketing and advertising carrier provider might also name those "automations", but what we're speaking approximately proper proper right here is a fixed-up in which an motion that is taken by means of the usage of the use of your electronic mail subscriber will reason a series of automated electronic mail messages to be despatched to that subscriber.

The cause I advise sequences as your starting point for imposing your monitoring is because of the reality those are links you need to installation as quickly as so one can continuously perform for you. All you need to do is ready apart 15-half-hour to exchange out your gift hyperlinks for added intentional ones so that you can higher tune your outcomes so you can enhance them shifting ahead. Better but, outsource the undertaking for your digital assistant. As a praise for this small investment into this one-time mission, you benefit insights that pay dividends as to how your sequences are acting for as long as you have got them walking.

Even if the concept of placing monitoring in region for each email you deliver is unbearable to you, this single try is well worth the everlong cross returned-on-investment it'll generate for you.

Let's take a look at a number of the most-used sequences in email marketing and advertising and how they're set up.

WELCOME SEQUENCES

A welcome series serves to introduce new e mail subscribers to you, your message and/or your gives via a sequence of emails. These are often called "nurture sequences" or "advent funnels". While you may convert to profits with this automation, the focal point of this electronic mail series leans extra toward building a relationship with your new subscriber.

Because you're introducing your self and your gives, this method is one of the unusual instances wherein your CAMPAIGN parameter is probably to trade and shift for the duration of the same promotional series.

For example, the number one e mail you deliver also can direct people for your podcast and highlight some precise episodes of hobby, at the equal time as your 2d electronic mail may additionally additionally communicate approximately a low-fee offer designed to get them a short win, at the identical time as your 3rd e mail asks them to sign up for your Facebook Group.

As such, your series may additionally furthermore appearance some element like this:

The format is as follows:

• CAMPAIGN = the offer you're directing internet site online web page site visitors to;

• MEDIUM = e-mail;

• SOURCE = I used "welcome" in the above example but you're welcome (pun supposed) to apply some thing else, together with "intro", "w-s", "nurture" - it's your call but all another time, the key is to be regular with something it's miles you select to use;

- CONTENT = which email in the collection is this.

Why hassle with the CONTENT parameter in case you're selling numerous things? Even notwithstanding the truth that the purpose and provide you're making for each e mail is fantastic on this series, there's charge in monitoring and seeing what the engagement is for logo spanking new subscribers over a chain of emails.

Are there nice hassle strains or calls-to-motion interior your welcome series which might be getting more love than others? Do you've got one provide that gets a deliver-load extra engagement than every unique? What form of content cloth cloth are your new subscribers maximum interested by? What makes them click on on, pretty literally?

We'll discover how you may enhance your Welcome Sequences in Module four but in advance than we get to optimization, we've a few extra sequences to map out.

SALES SEQUENCES

There are instances at the same time as someone symptoms and signs and symptoms up for your e-mail list for a selected offer or at the same time as your email subscriber takes a sure motion that suggests they're geared up, brought about or interested in a selected paid provide you have. I talk with those as "evergreen sequences" but you'll furthermore pay interest them being known as "sales series", "funnel automations" or any form of combination of these words. Whatever you choose to name them, those are the gathering of emails which might be despatched to a centered subscriber designed to educate your reader about a particular offer and the advantages it has in save for folks who buy it.

This is just like your welcome series besides that your CAMPAIGN parameter will usually be the same. After all, you'll be promoting the equal provide at some stage in the e-mail series and your SOURCE parameter will suggest that this is an evergreen collection in area of a welcome collection.

It may map out to some thing like this:

Its format might be:

- CAMPAIGN = your provide

- MEDIUM = e-mail;

- SOURCE = I used "ee" within the above instance as an acronym for Evergreen Email but as continuously, you may use a few issue you choose, so long as you're constant;

- CONTENT = which e-mail in the series that is.

That's the way you're capable of hone in on how each electronic mail of your evergreen series is appearing, like this:

We'll check making enjoy of those numbers greater within the next module, however I want you on the way to see and hook up with how this facts can be your first-rate optimization tool.

RE-ENGAGEMENT SEQUENCES

This series is the least amusing of all of the sequences. We flow into extra in-depth with trouble-taking photos unengaged subscribers with this series in Module 5 and talk what to do whilst your listing isn't engaged. However, I don't advise you fuss an excessive amount of over the tracking of this specific series because it isn't always probable to provide plenty price.

Your re-engagement series will yield one in each of 3 outcomes. Either your subscriber will:

1. Make the micro-willpower crucial to live on your list;

2. Confirm they want to unsubscribe from your listing; or

three. Their lack of interest and/or engagement will do you every the preference of getting you take away this character out of your touch listing.

There isn't hundreds to track or optimize right here and there's even less purpose to pursue doing so. It's a hint bit like agreeing to couple's remedy after the divorce papers are signed; your re-engagement collection IS the form of couple's therapy for you and your subscriber to see if it's feasible that there's something left to this relationship in advance than you end it and pass your separate strategies.

But as I see it, as soon as that courting is over, what are we seeking to enhance? The time and area to awareness on optimization Is with the folks that ARE attractive with you, and I should encourage you to make investments your interest and efforts with the parents which may be concerned and engaged with you.

EMAIL SIGNATURE BLOCK

Email advertising and advertising isn't confined to the emails you ship the use of your e-mail advertising and marketing and advertising services. I try and encourage my very very own subscribers to use the REPLY button and I make a addiction of studying and replying to genuinely all people who takes the day experience to study and respond to me. Fair is truthful, right?

Even in spite of the fact that I'm replying to truly one character as opposed to sending out a mass e mail, that respond notwithstanding the fact that includes e mail advertising and your signature block is an often-left out possibility to sell your gives.

The parameters I use for the ones are awesome-easy:

- CAMPAIGN = the provide name;

- MEDIUM = electronic mail;

- SOURCE = signature-block.

Unless I'm updating what I'm promoting, I in no manner update my signature block. For example, as quickly as I reply to an e mail, I in no way replace the CONTENT parameter to indicate the date I despatched the email. I don't do sufficient with this information to make it well really worth the strive it might require to replace every unmarried e-mail I send from my inbox.

The manner I music my e-mail signature block is ground stage, "inside the understand" shape of monitoring that I inspire you to put in location, however you moreover might also have my blessing to hold this goofy-smooth. If you find out your self searching at this records for your reviews and thinking about questions you want replied about your signature block engagement, that's while you're proudly owning your bossy pants and that it's time to replace your monitoring approach.

In truth, this is the crucial aspect to any tracking technique: at the same time as you located some awesome baseline tracking in location and accumulate the rewards of crystal-clear evaluations, you start asking your self questions about "I marvel if..." and "what if I had/knew/changed this one issue...".

This type of self-wondering is proof which you've hit your stride as a data-pushed boss. Why?

Because it way you inspired your personal dang self together with your non-public dang insights, and also you're asking yourself the varieties of boss mode questions so as to spark off you to show up as a higher model of your self primarily based totally on what you've already accomplished. Boom!

Chapter 4: Making Sense Of Your Email Traffic And Results

Once you're intentionally tracking your e mail marketing campaigns, you'll have devices of records you could use to decorate your effects:

• Your e mail advertising provider issuer will acquire records as to what's taking place with the actual emails themselves, which includes what number of human beings you despatched the email to within the first vicinity; and

• Your internet website analytics in order to inform you the tale of what your electronic mail subscribers did in your internet net web page after they clicked through at the emails you despatched.

Both of those are to be had to you and I inspire you to deal with them as separate however equally critical facts sources that play properly together.

Let's pop in an example to demonstrate the identical fee and significance of every, we may want to? Let's say you want to apprehend the conversion fee to sales of the very last electronic mail you sent out for your electronic mail list.

Unless you're the use of an all-in-one company like Kartra that still hosts your profits pages, your email advertising provider analytics are not going to document on how many income you made.

Meanwhile, in case you have a study the information your internet site analytics offers, it is able to can help you recognise how many income got here from e mail #6, but it can't let you know what number of humans obtained electronic mail #6.

In order to calculate your conversion charge to sales from email #6, you want to understand what number of human beings you sent e mail #6 to in addition to how many profits have been crafted from e mail #6. As such, that is a robust and common instance of whilst and why you will pass-reference the statistics furnished with the resource of way of your e-mail advertising and marketing provider to that furnished through your net web page analytics.

The brilliant issue higher than an instance with regards to knowledge a way to optimize your effects with records is to use case studies so permit's do some of the ones.

SEQUENCE CASE STUDIES

Since your Welcome Sequences are wherein most of your subscribers start, I determine it's a splendid sufficient vicinity for us to begin with information what our information is telling us as well.

LOOKING AT AND OPTIMIZING WELCOME SEQUENCES

Here are some internet website insights from our Welcome Sequence:

What we're capable of see right here is that e mail #1 is getting opened the maximum - this is regular - however it's also common in your engagement to lower chronologically. Yet, what we're seeing proper proper here is that e mail #2 isn't getting any love the least bit. In reality, it's no longer even displaying up in our opinions! Meanwhile, the remaining electronic mail inside the collection is seeing the subsequent-exceptional engagement fees… so what's up with that?

Let's peek at the gathering in query all mapped out:

In this example, email #2 emerge as a name-to-movement for the subscriber to answer and introduce themselves, so it makes feel that we're not seeing any engagement in our analytics because of the truth your subscribers did now not have a link to click on-through to our net page on this e-mail.

However, one observe our e-mail hassle lines gives us a few indication as to what else is going on right here:

Clearly we need to further check using emojis in trouble lines because it looks as if our goal market absolutely gravitates to the ones.

Our e-mail #five, in this situation, is a call-to-movement for a quiz we need to offer. Maybe it isn't the emojis which might be using higher engagement however it's truly the content cloth cloth we're selling.

Chapter 5: When Your Email Marketing Isn't Working

I like to mention "the begin is continuously a incredible vicinity to start" (due to the fact it's miles!) and almost about enhancing your email advertising and marketing efforts, the start does not start with what YOU are doing, however with what the era is doing.

EMAIL DELIVERABILITY

Before you exchange some difficulty collectively along with your approach to e-mail advertising and advertising and marketing, it's an first rate concept to take a look at your e mail deliverability. Email deliverability is a term used to explain the capability for an e mail which you send to attain an inbox to that you're sending it.

If your emails aren't even attaining the inbox, it doesn't absolutely undergo in thoughts what you convert due to the fact the larger problem that you need to restore first is probably your "sender recognition".

I understand, I apprehend - you idea your recognition became simply something you needed to fear approximately in excessive college. Alas, my promotional friend, your e-mail advertising and marketing self now has a sender reputation to worry approximately due to the fact this will and does impact your electronic mail deliverability.

There are severa reasons why your sender reputation can be impacted, together with junk mail complaints, bounce fees and the language you're the usage of to your situation lines. Another all-too-commonplace problem that can effect your deliverability is if you are sending emails that your list is constantly ignoring, email hosts will test that reason forget approximately you and a splendid way to thereby impact your popularity and deliverability.

So how do you discover what your sender popularity is and in which your email deliverability recognition stands? You can use a deliverability audit provider and you may locate an updated list of the services I suggest at book.Omgrowth.Com/e mail.

These services will assist you to run deliverability exams an awesome way to record on what varieties of troubles are being encountered and which e mail domains (i.E. @gmail.Com, @hotmail.Com, and masses of others.) are being impacted. This will permit you to higher understand your deliverability tendencies and most services will offer you with tool to enhance them.

I recommend which you run initial assessments:

1) Run one take a look at from right now in the inbox you typically use for emailing at once to at least one character; and

2) Run a 2nd take a look at from inside your email advertising and marketing carrier, as in case you were sending a manual out.

Why test emails from each locations? Because the emails you supply out of your inbox typically journey through awesome servers than the ones your e-mail advertising and marketing and advertising and marketing and advertising service uses and it's an excellent idea to get a sense for a manner every is acting.

However, even though you're sending two separate exams, try to use identical content material on each emails you're sending to lessen the unique motives why an e-mail might also moreover moreover or might not be delivered. Remember, your sender popularity and electronic mail deliverability IS impacted with the resource of the actual content cloth cloth and language you're using, and this is additionally why pretty a few electronic mail advertising offerings will have a SPAM Check/Verification previous to sending. As such, I endorse you try recycling a current e-e-newsletter you despatched to reflect "right" content cloth you may usually ship out.

Once you get hold of your reviews with the advocated adjustments and you're making the ones modifications, you can run every other set of audits to look the consequences of your upgrades.

You shouldn't count on to look a 100% rating and it in all likelihood gained't be simply worth the effort with a purpose to strive for that nice score, both. For instance, I'm not specially involved that the emails despatched to domain @yandex.Ru aren't being delivered; I do now not have any electronic mail subscribers who are registered with this area and I don't suspect I'm a large deal in Russia (that is what the top-degree area ".Ru" represents). I'm now not an Olympian and it isn't definitely surely really worth the try for me to are looking for out a amazing score the diverse Russian judges, and I encourage you to apply the identical sort of discernment as you assessment your very very own effects.

Since we're with regards to domains, despite the truth that, remember getting yours confirmed with the Google Postmaster, when you have no longer already completed so. This is kind of much like the equivalent of telling Google, "howdy! I'm running a completely expert enterprise over proper here!". Another perk is that once you're established, Google will at once-up gossip with you approximately the awful impacts taking place in your biz, like direct mail proceedings. You can go to postmaster.Google.Com for extra facts on getting your vicinity Google-tested.

Since @gmail.Com is probable to symbolize the very great percentage of addresses you ship emails to, verifying your area(s) is simply properly really worth the try to provide your emails the pleasant risk of being obtained in the Google-verse.

Once we've either eliminated or minimized electronic mail deliverability as an effect on our e mail campaigns, we are able to begin looking at unique problems we're encountering and artwork on enhancing the ones right away.

"I'M OVERWHELMED AND DON'T KNOW WHAT TO FOCUS ON!"

Fair. There's masses right here.

Let's first cope with the fact that we're speaking about marketing and advertising. This method there'll normally be a few factor to area up, song and beautify, and you'll in no manner be "completed". There isn't any doubt that those vibes will once in a while translate to emotions of crush and no longer feeling clean approximately what to interest on, in particular as your strategies and campaigns amplify and increase in complexity.

Having stated all that, right here's the sport plan I advocate in your electronic mail advertising and marketing optimization efforts:

1. Start with the resource of tagging your sequences;

2. Run an electronic mail deliverability take a look at to confirm your sender popularity and make certain you're getting into the proper inboxes;

three. As you time table and supply e-mail, make sure you're tagging your publicizes moving ahead; and

four. Create a quarterly dependancy of reviewing your e-mail advertising and advertising and marketing performance: have a take a look at and hone in on the dispositions taking place together together along with your sequences, repeat the way to your announces, and then zoom out even similarly to assess how e mail contributes to your ordinary general overall performance.

And endure in thoughts the next few questions as little helpers designed to direct you want air internet website site visitors manipulate toward what you should take a look at based on what is happening (or now not taking region, in a few cases!) together with your e-mail advertising and advertising.

"PEOPLE AREN'T CLICKING ON MY LINKS!"

If you aren't satisfied with what number of humans are clicking via on the links you're embedding for your emails, undergo in mind checking yourself. I'm now not being sassy, each - I suggest this sincerely: open your emails and feature a have a look at your links.

- Is it obvious that those are hyperlinks? Are they super hues and are they underlined in each other manner from the rest of the text?

Are your links seen, clean-to-discover and frequently displayed?

● Are your calls-to-motion (CTAs) strong, easy and compelling?

● Have you tested your links on computing device, mobile AND pill to make sure they artwork on all devices and spot if there's some factor that can be superior about those precise consumer opinions?

● Are you sending the same emails in your complete list? Would there be a benefit to in addition segmenting your listing and converting the messaging interior your emails to speak for your subscribers in a extra direct, customized way?

● Are you giving your people an possibility to talk out approximately the campaigns they're NOT interested in listening to approximately?

This ultimate one is vital and in my opinion, it is an ignored tactic of e-mail advertising. We noted this in the "Getting Your Emails Read" section of Module 1 but it bears repeating: offer your people the opportunity to talk up approximately what they don't need to pay attention about with the aid of providing them with the functionality to determine-out of promotions they aren't interested in.

Not simplest do you not want to train your e-mail subscribers to disregard you after they aren't interested by a proposal you're selling, but when you have a devoted internet web page net web page which you typically ship humans to after they do pick to determine-out of a particular vending, you're then able to hone in on which offers human beings are maximum probable to choose out from.

To do this, you'll clean out the internet net page in that you automatically redirect subscribers who pick out-from your promotions to, and then look up your CAMPAIGN parameter to appearance in which each of your gives stand on this regard.

Another method could be to clearly disassociate yourself out of your popularity as a marketer and approach your content with easy eyes.

Examine your state of affairs traces and be aware about the primary line of textual content that suggests up inside the inbox, after which ask your self, "Would I click on on on that? Am I offering a compelling purpose to open this e-mail? Am I connecting with my purpose market on this undertaking line?"

If you aren't fantastic, it may be properly really worth locating out one-of-a-type trouble traces to simply see what does and does not connect to your subscribers.

ABOUT SPLIT-TESTING

Sometimes known as "A/B sorting out", split-sorting out is the workout of publishing multiple model of a advertising and advertising asset a very good manner to look and take a look at what your target audience responds fantastic to. While it's far once in a while used on net websites and touchdown pages to test such things as replica, positioning, shades or photograph usage, amongst particular topics, maximum electronic mail advertising provider carriers will allow you to moreover cut up-test your electronic mail state of affairs lines and/or content material cloth to appearance if version A outperforms model B.

A phrase of caution earlier than we get into the way to break up-test your e-mail trouble lines: this optimization method shouldn't additionally be on your radar if you're sending the e-mail to a great deal much less than 2000 electronic mail subscribers.

Why? Because that's what you want to paintings with on the manner to start seeing big consequences. Think about it: model A of your e mail will go to one thousand subscribers whilst version B is going to some other a thousand subscribers. Since we are able to no longer depend upon open expenses as an engagement metric, we'll need to popularity on click on on on-through prices, it's why you need at least one thousand humans whose behaviors and options you're measuring.

With the ones numbers, allow's say version A of your electronic mail has a click on-through charge of four.Five%, because of this that 45 people clicked through; in the intervening time, model B has a click on-thru rate of 6.2%, due to this that sixty two human beings clicked via.

While version B outperforms model A through 1.7%, we're talking about absolutely 17 human beings and the statistical relevance of those smaller gadgets of numbers makes it tough to benefit dependable insights and make any real picks about your advertising and effects.

Hence why I advocate 2000 subscribers due to the fact the absolute minimum list duration you want to be running with in case you're going to interrupt up-check your state of affairs traces. If your listing size is smaller than that, the optimization techniques you'd maximum benefit from are those who recognition extra on list boom and growing engagement earlier than you make investments your effort and time into finding out.

With that disclaimer out of the manner, there may be greater to have a take a look at than absolutely click on-through costs as you'll likely be testing some earnings emails as properly. As such, you'll want to have a take a look at your conversion expenses and what diploma of engagement each electronic mail is getting when they click on on-through to your net website.

You ought to use the UTM parameter for CONTENT to help recognize which model of the e-mail we're assessing the general general performance for. Let's say you're using the date as the CONTENT parameter, you could do "&utm_content=20230630-a" and "&utm_content=20230630-b" to appearance what the overall performance is for the individuals who clicked-thru on version A as opposed to version B of the emails you sent on June thirtieth, 2023 (or 2023-06-30).

To well cut up-test, you'll want to get downright scientific approximately what you're trying out and pass into your take a look at with a hypothesis. You recollect when you did technological expertise experiments in college, right? You normally started with a hypothesis you have been taking off to reveal or disprove.

Same address cut up-trying out!

Examples are our pals so allow's use one we commenced out earlier however didn't art work thru but: permit's say we expect that our subscribers might be greater interested by our emails when we use emojis interior the issue line. As such, for the subsequent zone, we're commiting to cut up-finding out every email we supply over the next three months with issue traces that incorporate emojis as opposed to ones that don't.

"But Lanie," you

 can be saying. "That's hundreds of electronic mail!" Yes, as regular with regular, you're accurate and this is lots of e mail. But that's the factor: we want to have sufficient assessments and outcomes to make a few accurate assessments about our speculation.

This is likewise why we need to undertake a naming convention to find out our emoji state of affairs lines (model A) and our non-emoji hassle lines (model B) to make certain we're evaluating everyday effects. A little #protip in case you foresee this being tough: truly because it's known as A/B Testing doesn't advocate that's how you want to pick out out your campaigns. If it's much less difficult which will use an obvious parameter like "&utm_content=20230630-emoji" and "&utm_content=20230630-noemoji", then try this. After all, you're the boss, apple sauce, and it's your call to make the exquisite picks for you and the way you want to function and marketplace.

Once you wrap up your sector and also you're doing all of your quarterly assessment, you'll set some time aside to assess your results. It's a great concept to start with your e-mail advertising company analytics to look if you could choose out any sort of patterns or trends along side your click on-thru expenses. I encourage you to observe your open costs, too

, and see if something important pops out at you. Even despite the fact that your open prices aren't a dependable metric, they're in addition unreliable in this example so it doesn't harm to take a look at them, even if we aren't making any final selections on the ones numbers. We're not going to make any selections based mostly on those numbers but it's form of like window-shopping at Bergdorf Goodman at the holidays; you're now not purchasing for or investing some issue into what you're seeing but you never apprehend if it'll inspire some component for you.

Make be aware of some factor that receives your hobby - specifically if there are unique e-mail devices that stand out to you - in advance than you circulate onto your net internet site analytics to look how every e-mail scenario behaves and interacts along side your offers and content material.

The example we used modified into trying out using emojis in the task traces but there are a whole lot of various topics you may test to your hassle traces as nicely. Here are a few great problem line-associated content material you can keep in mind checking out:

- The use of passive voice (like, "state of affairs strains you'll love") versus active voice (like, "you'll love the ones mission traces");

- The use of personalization (like, "Lanie, open this now") rather than non-customized (like, "You have to open this now");

- The use of punctuation (like, "did this?" in place of "I clearly have to inform you this!");

- The use of captions for urgency (like, "[TIME SENSITIVE] Check this out" in choice to "Today best: Check this out");

- The use of intimate language (like, "See you day after today?") instead of expert language (like, "Sign up for the next day's workshop");

- The use of interest phrases on the facet of "now", "unfastened", and so forth.

Keep in mind that I am now not a copywriter and don't faux to be an professional at trouble lines (in spite of the reality that during case you visit ebook.Omgrowth.Com/e mail, you'll find my recommendations for sources from folks that are and who I receive as real with to help me with my very non-public email duplicate if that could be a area you're on the lookout for to decorate).

My motive in sharing those is to get your wheels turning with what is available for you to test. Another issue is that no matter the truth that we've been speaking approximately difficulty strains, there's an entire lot greater you can A/B take a look at to your emails than genuinely state of affairs strains. You also can test that first line of preview text that shows up inside the email header, which shows up inside the inbox like this:

You can cut up-check the language or duplicate you're the usage of for your actual emails, or the colors of your hyperlinks and buttons, or the varieties of pix you're the usage of in the emails, and of route, as long as you're getting enough website on-line site visitors to make the consequences well honestly worth it, you may moreover split-check your automations and evergreen sequences as nicely.

The e mail optimization international is truely your oyster but a phrase of warning: stick to finding out clearly one issue at a time to make certain you have got barriers as to what your outcomes are and to ensure you have clean insights that you're assessing.

And preserve in mind that your insights are imagined to be parlayed. This method that you can and want to boom the inclinations and patterns you're seeing together with your emails into distinctive regions. For instance, if you're seeing a few issue that works in your e mail situation strains, have a look at how that facts can be completed for your social media captions, your income replica, your marketing campaigns, and more. The better your statistics is ready what your humans interact with and the manner they have interaction together along with your content material cloth and offers, the much less tough it's far to use that statistics to see better advertising and marketing consequences in amazing areas as properly.

"PEOPLE ARE UNSUBSCRIBING. LIKE, A LOT!"

When you placed loads art work into developing your email listing, it cannot continuously FEEL like human beings unsubscribing from your e-mail list is a terrific element… but it can be. If humans aren't choosing up what you're throwing down or perhaps they have got discovered out

all they'll be interested by from you, they're definitely doing you a choice via putting off themselves as someone who you've got a few detail useful to share with. After all, you ARE shopping for those subscribers via your e mail advertising and advertising and advertising services fees and those aren't like souvenirs that you want to hang right away to.

Having said that, you don't want to be seeing extra than 2% of your listing unsubscribing at a time on a regular foundation because it typically method some thing isn't always proper. If the ones unsubscribes are discovered with SPAM lawsuits, this is specifically vital for you to test out; if humans are reporting you as SPAM, this may effect your sender recognition and email deliverability.

Here are a few areas you can take a look at to help restriction your unsubscribe expenses and SPAM lawsuits, in addition to a few move-to questions to advantage a few insights on what exactly you can work directly to beautify this:

YOUR SUBSCRIPTION PROCESS

• How are people getting onto your listing? Are they signing up for your offers deliberately or do you have got human beings signing up who don't definitely apprehend what they'll be agreeing to gather from you?

• Is the messaging you are the usage of to get humans to your listing similar to what you operate as speedy as those human beings are to your listing, or must there be a "disconnect" amongst what your subscriber's expectancies are and what you surely deliver?

YOUR TAGGING PROCESS

• Are you segmenting your subscribers in a way that is presenting them with emails and content cloth applicable to the pursuits they have for being in your list?

• Is there a manner you could be more precise with the way you're tagging your subscribers' interests and motives for being for your list so that you can higher in form their desires with the emails you're sending?

YOUR EMAIL DELIVERY

• If you've got got a couple of automated e mail sequences walking, is it feasible that they overlap every one of a kind and also you're overwhelming your new subscribers and/or clients with too many emails and conflicting promotions or messaging?

• If you're running a specific advertising and also you're sending greater emails than you typically do, it's miles normal to appearance your unsubscribe expenses upward thrust sooner or later of this era. But are you giving those who aren't interested by this specific vending and/or provide the opportunity to opt-out of that series whilst however being able to stay in your electronic mail listing and hold receiving correspondence after this promo?

● Also, undergo in mind reviewing the frequency of your email delivery. In this situation, you'll need to perform a bit fee-gain assessment with the aid of no longer first rate focusing on your unsubscribe costs but searching at the type of sales and/or engagement that the ones identical emails generated as properly.

YOUR ACTUAL EMAIL CONTENT

● Similar to the final issue, you don't need to assess an email definitely toward its unsubscribe costs; you need to evaluate the general universal overall performance, together with click on on on-throughs and income or engagement generated. You're seldom capable of take a look at one metric in isolation and function it inform the complete story of your trendy performance, and you could need to have a have a look at the "big photo" of what happened to understand if it's the actual content material fabric of your emails that want to be modified.

● We talked about split-attempting out your mission traces earlier however you can also split-check the real kinds of content fabric material on your emails. Do your humans reply better to video? Do they determine upon prolonged-shape emails or shorter ones? Have you tested the usage of GIFs and photographs in place of textual content-best?

There's a purpose why nearly each e mail advertising and advertising provider integrates trying out alternatives into its systems; all marketing and advertising is a constant wash-rinse-repeat manner of testing, assessing and enhancing how we're promoting ourselves, our messages and our offers.

We're regularly so focused on getting extra web web page web site traffic and further subscribers that we neglect the optimization opportunities we already have to collect on our cutting-edge listing. As such, improving our e mail advertising and marketing overall performance isn't constantly our first precedence, in spite of the fact that it could result in the maximum vital returns.

"MY SUBSCRIBERS AREN'T SUPER-ENGAGED!"

This is in which your target market is channeling Tracy Chapman and they're asking you to "supply me one cause to live right here"; if your subscribers aren't doing something with your emails however similarly they'll be no longer unsubscribing, it's because of the fact there's despite the fact that a touch "a few element-some element" there, and it's up to you to do something excellent about that.

YOUR RE-ENGAGEMENT SEQUENCE

There are masses of factors to do not forget and pretty some strategies you could take. Regardless of the way you go about "selecting your very very personal adventure" with this, there is probably 3 stages to your re-engagement collection:

- Identifying unengaged subscribers;

- Giving your subscribers the opportunities and incentives to re-interact; and

- Re-assessing your dating collectively together with your subscribers.

STEP 1: IDENTIFY UNENGAGED SUBSCRIBERS

There are hundreds of processes to do this, which incorporates putting in place automations internal your email advertising and marketing issuer with the intention to understand your unengaged subscribers on your behalf and ship them through an automation series. I inspire you to publish a rate rate tag or are seeking out thru your electronic mail advertising and marketing corporation's records base to look how they recommend placing this up as the tech set-up for this could range for each platform.

I choose to do that manually for a couple of legitimate motives:

1) I'm a manage freak. There, I stated it. But I don't like having a few aspect as critical as re-attractive my subscribers show up on automobile-pilot. I need to have a say about whilst the ones sequences exit, and I am strategic approximately once they do.

For example, it would pressure me bonkers to recognise that on Day 2 of a launch or advertising and marketing, a person obtained 2 promotional emails but then became automatically entered right right right into a re-engagement series that basically said "hello! Why don't you open the ones? Do you wanna split?".

Because those emails are strategically designed to get subscribers to open them, possibilities are they will. But to have a person have interaction with one of the re-engagement emails and spot that I had despatched proper away it following 2 hard pitch emails right in advance than that doesn't sit down properly with me. This is my opinion however once I located myself in the feature of the subscriber, I don't just like the optics of having a profits e mail on Day 1, each different income e-mail on Day 2 and then a "don't you wanna live in touch email" exit on Day 3. It consists of a peculiar "toddler please" vibe that does not mirror how I want to speak to and be seen via my intention market.

2) I need to combine re-engagement sequences as part of my quarterly assessment. I'm generally clocking in my list growth price within the meanwhile anyways, so I discover it to be an inexperienced use of 15-20 mins to additionally have a examine which emails received the pinnacle engagement during the last three months, which of them acquired the lowest engagement, and the way those evaluate to my past overall performance. This is wherein I pick out what went nicely this sector so I can do more of that, what didn't flow as well so I can make certain I'm doing less of that, and discover what outcomes I'm less high-quality approximately that could use a chunk extra attempting out.

This is likewise wherein I will segment the subscribers who have not been attractive with my emails this area: are there any dispositions or patterns I can turn out to be aware of, and what number of my e mail list are we speakme approximately right here?

I will then decide as soon as I will initiate my re-engagement collection for the ones subscribers, based totally totally on my promotional calendar. If I'm sparkling off a heavy merchandising time desk, I'll generally maintain off a hint - as a minimum in keeping with week or - or if I'm headed proper into a promotional duration, I'll make reminder notes in my calendar or time table a undertaking in my challenge control gadget as to as quickly as I need to provoke this.

STEP 2: TAG AND RE-ENGAGE

Whether you select to use automations otherwise you're manually beginning this sequence primarily based completely to your promotional calendar, you want to make certain you tag your subscriber as someone who has gone via your re-engagement series at the same time as you flow down that route.

Why?

Because you need to have a manner of identifying whether you have already been through this situation of making up and breaking aside and making up again.

If they've already received your re-engagement collection and that they recommit to your listing the number one time, but then weren't attractive over again, it's likely time you tried something else. You likely won't want to ship an appropriate identical hassle as you probably did final time as that in reality emerge as a brief and quite useless answer however proper right here's an idea: email them for my part in choice to the use of pre-written templates or automations. Maybe pass the more mile and create a brief customized video message the usage of a carrier like Loom or Bonjoro. You can remind them of why they initially signed up for your electronic mail list and ask them how you could higher meet them in which they may be or if there's some thing you may assist with.

This can be a exquisite possibility for actual connection and feedback as to how often you're sending emails, what styles of gives humans want from you, and the manner you'll be more attractive with human beings on your list. Sure, it's extra paintings, but going the more mile normally is and that's what places you in addition beforehand than maximum.

However, your number one re-engagement series will typically be made from 3 or so emails designed to see if there's however any hobby in advance than you unsubscribe this character from your listing.

There are 2 strategies you could technique your re-engagement collection:

1) You can send a conga line of "properly day! You haven't opened my emails in a while" emails advising them that they'll be robotically removed in the event that they don't interact together with your emails. These are right now-beforehand calls-to-movement that may

artwork well with the right target audience who simply need a touch nudge; or

2) You can also send what I name a "opposite welcome series" and as the decision indicates, it'll basically be your welcome collection being despatched in a opposite order.

One manner to technique welcome sequences is to ship one email introduction pronouncing a touch some problem about how you and brand serve your purpose marketplace, then an creation to your offers, and then a few sort of mini-survey wherein subscribers can self-understand their hobbies so that you can tag and serve those humans in line with their stated interests.

Your contrary welcome series is trying to set up a bit micro-determination out of your reader so you'll start via the use of sending this sort of surveys asking your reader to will permit you to recognize what they want from you. After all, everyone's desired subject matter is themselves just so's an first rate area to begin validating whether or not or no longer you and the reader have whatever to offer each different. Then remind them of your paid and/or unfastened offers and ultimately, contrary-introduce yourself and ask your subscriber if there's a few element at the manner to offer them in advance than unsubscribing them.

While the intention is re-engagement, I might also make it clean for them to unsubscribe inside the occasion that they aren't fascinated. After all, self-choice should consist of the choice of "nope, we're performed right here, thanks for the recollections."

STEP three: ASSESS YOUR RELATIONSHIP STATUS

You've despatched out your re-engagement collection… now what? Well, now we wait. Give it a few days and perhaps even every week or in advance than you start mechanically unsubscribing humans from your listing as they'll be on excursion or pass into their inbox best once in a while.

However, I could make sure not to deliver them whatever else until they've each re-engaged otherwise you've unsubscribed them; once more, it's approximately the optics of pronouncing "appropriate day! Do you continue to wanna be buddies" and then not looking ahead to or acknowledging the answer - and silence IS a solution - in advance than sending them extra profits emails.

If no clicks come through with this series, you can unsubscribe them yourself with one caveat: if they have sold from you, I should recommend that you make sure you've got got lists and segments in your merchandise which may be reduce loose the list of subscribers you market to. You need to notwithstanding the reality that satisfy the get entry to to merchandise they paid for and characteristic a way of providing them with updates on their purchases.

If Email Marketing Optimization appears heavy, it's because of the fact there's hundreds this is going into your own electronic mail advertising optimization and this e-book covers an entire lot of that floor.

And right proper right here's the kicker: you're in no manner going to be executed with any of this. All virtual advertising and marketing is a wash-rinse-repeat tool of publishing, tracking and improving, and then taking what you've determined to publish, song and beautify, all all once more.

While your e mail listing is generally your maximum engaged site site visitors deliver, HOW engaged they're is clearly as lots as you. You have a duty inside the path of these adorable human beings who have located their trust and talk to information for your fingers.

Try to continually preserve in thoughts what a privilege it's far as a manner to have and foster this courting together with your subscribers, and that like every relationships, you need to do the entirety you could to make the advantages mutual and to supply those advantages as frequently as possible.

Chapter 6: Action

1. Paging Falcon

Subject Line: RE: Paging Falcon?

Maybe the above e-mail situation line doesn't interest you inside the least, that's comprehensible.

But what if you had been like my prospect and worked at a organisation wherein nicknames are the whole thing?

Your paintings nickname will become your name in actual life. You genuinely have an avatar that goes on the side of it.

This nickname will become a powerful scenario line and a high-quality way to get your cold email opened and observe.

Now it's your flip. Start to exercise right here.

Cold e-mail prompt:

Can you find out your prospect's nickname? Now provide you with a 10 thoughts of the manner you may use the man or woman's nickname on your problem line.

1.

2.

3.

4.

5.

6.

7.

8.

9.

10.

2. The Afterlife or Life After?

Subject Line: RE: Life after Oculus?

I don't don't forget people spend masses time thinking about what will arise to them after they die. Then another time I may be incorrect. Maybe it is simply me who thinks this manner?

However, I do assume that people spend a high-quality deal of time considering beyond jobs they've got held, art work they loved, and what sort of artwork they want to do next.

Why now not ask your prospect approximately her paintings "afterlife"?

Let's keep the exercising once more now. It is your turn.

Cold email set off:

What are 10 tactics or thoughts you may use to invite approximately the life they preference to guide after their present day corporation.

1. Life after x?

2.

three.

four.

5.

6.

7.

eight.

nine.

10.

3. What Courses Are You Taking?

Subject Line: RE: New Computer Vision Exercises

Computer imaginative and prescient and tool mastering are famous buzzwords on the subject of era nowadays. Have you heard of them in advance than? Maybe this is the primary time you are taking note of them.

Are you a pc vision professional?

No, likely now not if you are analyzing this e-book. It's k, I am now not one each.

Sometimes I warfare to understand how this new era is going to alternate our global. Luckily there are those who understand the ability.

And there are also human beings like my prospect who love to have a examine more approximately the difficulty and feature a study it for amusing.

Now it's your flip. How are you taking element in this workout?

Cold e-mail prompt:

Find which Coursera guides your prospect has been taking and use these on your issue line. Or even discover the github repos he/she follows and use them for your message.

Write down 10 approaches you operate the ones to create an wonderful assignment line or cold e mail.

1.

2.

three.

four.

five.

6.

7.

8.

nine.

10.

4. Tweets From Customers

Subject Line: RE: Autopilot is arriving over the air, of route I am so jealous.

I encounter a large quantity of statistics on line for my opportunities. Sometimes too much facts, and I find out greater about their private lives than I would like to apprehend.

I positioned that one in every of my prospects tweeted the above assertion in the task line at Tesla's Twitter account.

I ended up which incorporates a picture of his tweet in my cold e mail along side a question or for him.

His reaction, "Woa! Awesome recruiting e mail!"

And the conversation flowed from there.

Now it's your flip.

Cold electronic mail activate:

Come up with 10 mind wherein you can patch together your corporation or product along with your prospect's hobbies. (Feel loose to cheat and discover this statistics on their blog, twitter feed, or instagram.)

I'll offer you with the first one. My prospect became tweeting about stage 1 car automation, so I used the scenario line below.

1. Robot motors?

2.

3.

4.

5.

6.

7.

eight.

nine.

10.

five. Recommendations

Subject Line: RE: If I have to clone [redacted]... I surely might probable

Cloning became a hot topic a few years back. I don't seem to listen as an lousy lot approximately it anymore. Maybe now researchers and scientists clone people and animals without discussing it?

I don't understand. I don't observe the records that carefully so it is probably my fault.

My possibilities, as a substitute, are each unique story, and I pay near interest to them.

I observed a recommendation a functionality candidate acquired on LinkedIn wherein the man or woman recommending them used the above word.